# Open My Eyes

*The Daily Search for Wondrous Things*

Volume 1

**Jason Hardin**

*Open My Eyes: The Daily Search for Wondrous Things* (Vol. 1)
© 2022 by DeWard Publishing Company, Ltd.
P.O. Box 290696, Tampa, FL 33687
www.deward.com

Cover by nvoke design.

The preponderance of Bible quotations are taken from the The Holy Bible, English Standard Version®, copyright © 2001 by Crossway Bibles, a publishing ministry of Good News Publishers. Used by permission. All rights reserved. Any emphasis in Bible quotations is added.

Reasonable care has been taken to trace original sources for any excerpts and quotations appearing in this book and to document such information. For material not in the public domain, fair use standards and practices were followed. Should any attribution be found to be incorrect or incomplete, the publisher welcomes written documentation supporting correction for subsequent printing.

Printed in the United States of America.

ISBN: 978-1-947929-20-3

**For Jadyn.**

God heard, and we are forever thankful.

May the simple reflections in this little book remind you that he continues to hear, and that he is good.

All the time.

# TABLE OF CONTENTS

## Week Eight

## Week Nine

## Week Ten

# Preface

Every once in a while, someone will ask, "If you had one piece of advice to give for spiritual growth and health, what would it be?" For a long time, I didn't know how to answer that question. In recent years, my response has been straightforward and simple: start your day, every day, reading something from God's word. Nothing has helped me more. I don't believe any one thing has helped the brothers and sisters in the local churches I've been blessed to serve more than reading a little bit of God's word every day. The Son of God knew what he was talking about when he emphasized, "Man shall not live by bread alone, but by every word that comes from the mouth of God." I've tried to take those words seriously.

Since 2008, I've been jotting down simple reflections on my daily Bible readings. I've tried to keep them brief, heartfelt, and practical in hopes that they might be of some encouragement to my daughters in the years to come. I never really had any intention of publishing them in a book, but as the collection has grown (and I've arrived at that point in my life where I'm thinking more and more about what I can leave behind as a blessing to others), this series of devotionals has grown to feel like a real contribution I can make. More often than not, I've written with my daughters in mind and, if the Lord wills, their eventual children and grandchildren. The process has been an immeasurable blessing to me. Perhaps the fruit of the process will be a blessing to you as well.

I've found praying Psalm 119.18 to be helpful any time I open God's word—"Open my eyes, that I may behold wondrous things out of your law." With that verse in mind, we've called this series *The Daily Search for Wondrous Things.* The approach is a little different than your typical big book of 365 readings, one for each day of the year. There are no calendar dates, just weekday names (Sunday, Monday, etc.), which means these little books can be picked up and started at any point throughout the year. The readings flow each week in a simple pattern:

- **Sundays:** a reflection from the Psalms
- **Mondays, Wednesdays, and Fridays:** reflections from the Old Testament
- **Tuesdays, Thursdays, and Saturdays:** reflections from the New Testament

In Isaiah 55.10–11, the LORD said:

> For as the rain and the snow that come down from heaven
>     and do not return there but water the earth,
> making it bring forth and sprout,
>     giving seed to the sower and bread to the eater,
> so shall my word be that goes out from my mouth;
>     it shall not return to me empty,
> but it shall accomplish that which I purpose,
>     and shall succeed in the thing for which I sent it.

I believe that promise with all of my heart. God's word is amazing. It's living and active. Our Father's purpose for his word *will* be realized.

May we have hearts that are open to its life-changing power. May these simple reflections provide you a little more fuel for the journey. Most of all, may we walk with Jesus each and every day, every step of the way.

In his footsteps, the best is always yet to come.

# WEEK ONE

## SUNDAY

### *He is Awesome; Come and See*

Come and see what God has done:
he is awesome in his deeds toward the children of man.
(Psa 66.5)

"Come and see." What an invitation! "Come and see what God has done." Isn't this the invitation extended to all of us on this, the Lord's day? Take a moment to think about how many elements of our assembling together revolve around this amazing, ancient invitation.

As we address one another in psalms, hymns, and spiritual songs, isn't this what we're singing to each other?

Come and see what God has done:
he is awesome in his deeds toward the children of man.

As we bow our heads and a brother in Christ leads us before the throne of God above in prayer, isn't this the essence of "Our Father in heaven, hallowed be your name"?

Come and see what God has done:
he is awesome in his deeds toward the children of man.

As we open our Bibles and listen to the preaching of God's word, isn't this the heartbeat of the faithful herald of the gospel?

Come and see what God has done:
  he is awesome in his deeds toward the children of man.

As we observe the Lord's Supper and remember the angel's announcement to the women at the tomb...

"Do not be afraid, for I know that you seek Jesus who was crucified. He is not here, for he has risen, as he said. Come, see the place where he lay." (Matt 28.5–6)

...what an invitation, extended centuries before that tomb found empty at dawn on the first day of the week...

Come and see what God has done:
  he is awesome in his deeds toward the children of man.

...an invitation that continues to be extended—to you, to me, to everyone—on this, the Lord's day.

He is awesome. Come and see.

# MONDAY

## *Full Eyes, Empty Hearts*

"On the day when I chose Israel, I swore to the offspring of the house of Jacob, making myself known to them in the land of Egypt; I swore to them, saying, 'I am the LORD your God.' On that day I swore to them that I would bring them out of the land of Egypt into a land that I had searched out for them, a land flowing with milk and honey, the most glorious of all lands." (Ezek 20.5–6)

God wanted what was best for Israel in every sense of the word. He chose them. He made himself known to them, entering into a covenant with them as I AM WHO I AM. He liberated them from slavery and provided the most glorious of all lands.

"And I said to them, 'Cast away the detestable things your eyes feast on, every one of you, and do not defile yourselves with the idols of Egypt; I am the LORD your God.'" (Ezek 20.7)

Take a moment to think about your Creator's description of idols in that verse—"detestable things your eyes feast on"—tempting things, alluring things, enticing things that provide quick hits of gratification for our eyes ... and defile our hearts in the process. **Israel missed out on the best because they allowed their eyes to feast on what ultimately left their hearts empty.**

"I gave them my statutes and made known to them my rules, by which, if a person does them, he shall live...that they might know that I am the LORD who sanctifies them. But the house of Israel rebelled against me in the wilderness. They did not walk in my statutes but rejected my rules, by which, if a person does them, he shall live." (Ezek 20.11–13)

And thousands of years later, we continue to find ourselves at essentially the same crossroads. All day, every day, our eyes are invited to feast on the pixelated delicacies abundantly supplied by the idols of money, sex, power, and success. A near-infinite supply of attention-sucking appetizers is constantly available at our fingertips and as long as we are willing to scroll, click, or sit through another recommended video, the opportunities to feast our eyes will continue.

**It has never been easier to live with full eyes and empty hearts.**

But our Creator still wants what is best for us in every sense of the word. He desires authentic relationship with us. He is willing and able to liberate us, transform and mature us, use us for good, and provide the most glorious of all inheritances.

"I gave them my statutes and made known to them my rules, by which, if a person does them, he shall live…"

Tucked in Ezekiel 20 is a reminder I need from the start of this new week. Guard your heart. Make a covenant with your eyes. Evaluate the source and substance of your affections. Think about the best use of your time. It's going to take deliberate effort and God-shaped focus to look past the easy feasts and empty cultural calories that will waste so much of your energy and leave your heart empty by the end of the week. But if you will delight yourself in the LORD, meditate on his precepts, and walk in his statutes, your heart will be full.

And you will live.

# TUESDAY

## *A Clear View of Him Who is Invisible*

When we live with full eyes and empty hearts, assurance runs low and conviction wears thin. It's hard to hope from an empty heart.

When we simply go with the flow of the world—walking and talking and acting and feeling by sight—there will always be plenty to keep our eyes full, but it's hard to build conviction for things that are never granted my undivided attention. So prayer takes a backseat to the next Netflix episode, Bible reading gets pushed to the back burner of tomorrow, I'll find the margin to worship on the weekend (as long as my eyes aren't too full of other, more pressing things) ... and I wonder in those dark nights of the soul why I'm struggling to hope with assurance and trust with conviction.

Hebrews 11 reminds us in the form of some powerful examples to look up from the cares and riches and pleasures of life to what cannot be seen with our physical eyes. Consider:

> Abraham obeyed when he was called to go out to a place that he was to receive as an inheritance. And he went out, not knowing where he was going. By faith he went to live in the land of promise, as in a foreign land, living in tents with Isaac and Jacob, heirs with him of the same promise. (11.8–9)

Why? Why do such a thing?

For **he was looking forward** to the city that has foundations, whose designer and builder is God. (11.10)

Example after example is offered in Hebrews 11 of men and women who hoped with assurance and trusted with conviction. They lived by and died with faith in God's promises, "**having seen them** and greeted them from afar" (11.13).

By faith Joseph, at the end of his life, made mention of the exodus of the Israelites and gave directions concerning his bones. (11.22)

Joseph could "see" something that wouldn't happen in space and time for centuries.

By faith Moses, when he was grown up, refused to be called the son of Pharaoh's daughter, choosing rather to be mistreated with the people of God than to enjoy the fleeting pleasures of sin. He considered the reproach of Christ greater wealth than the treasures of Egypt, for **he was looking** to the reward. (11.24–26)

"He was looking." In an era where most eyes were full of the gold and glitter of the Pharaohs, Moses lifted his eyes from the fleeting to focus on the eternal. And what came as a result? His heart wasn't empty. His hope was sure. His conviction was strong. By faith, he was equipped to endure "**as seeing** him who is invisible" (11.27).

A clear view of him who is invisible. Think about that today. What could possibly be worth more?

# WEDNESDAY

## *Make a Beginning*

**42,360.**

> These were the people of the province who came up out of the captivity of those exiles whom Nebuchadnezzar the king of Babylon had carried captive to Babylonia. They returned to Jerusalem and Judah. (Ezra 2.1)

42,360 came home to no houses, no walls, no gates, no altar, no temple. How easy would it have been to surrender to despair? How tempting to fixate on "the good old days" to the point of accomplishing nothing in the present?

I love the language in Ezra 3.8:

> Now in the second year after their coming to the house of God at Jerusalem, in the second month, Zerubbabel the son of Shealtiel and Jeshua the son of Jozadak **made a beginning**, together with the rest of their kinsmen, the priests and the Levites and all who had come to Jerusalem from the captivity.

Ordinary people "made a beginning." How? There was a first step. The first appointed priest. A first sacrifice. The first assignment. A first foundation stone. The first song. Ordinary people "made a beginning."

You don't have to wait until January 1 to make a beginning. Is there something in your life that needs attention? Some relationship that needs healing? What about your walk with Jesus? Your family? Your habits? Is there something of real (maybe even *eternal*) significance that's being neglected? Some sin that needs to be crucified and left behind?

Maybe "making a beginning" begins with an apology. A confession. Repentance. Letting those who care about you know that everything isn't okay. Asking for help. Prioritizing. Less _____, more_____. Less complaining, more gratitude. Less wasting, more intentionality. Less procrastinating, more participating.

Yesterday is gone and tomorrow isn't guaranteed, but the steadfast love and mercies of the Lord are new this morning (Lam 3.22–23). Maybe today is a good day to make a beginning.

# THURSDAY

## *Fulfillment Walked Among Us*

All this took place **to fulfill** what the Lord had spoken
by the prophet.... (Matt 1.22)

When something has been *fulfilled*, it's been put into effect. Re-
quirements have been satisfied. Standards have been realized. Full
potential has been met.

*The Gospel According to Matthew* is full of fulfillments. From
beginning to end, this tax collector whose life was forever
changed by the son of a carpenter is pointing his readers to the
accomplishments of Jesus, and what it all ultimately means.

> But as [Joseph] considered these things, behold, an angel of the
> Lord appeared to him in a dream, saying, "Joseph, son of David, do
> not fear to take Mary as your wife, for that which is conceived in
> her is from the Holy Spirit. She will bear a son, and you shall call
> his name Jesus, for he will save his people from their sins." **All this
> took place to fulfill what the Lord had spoken by the prophet:**
>
> "Behold, the virgin shall conceive and bear a son, and they shall
> call his name Immanuel" (which means, God with us). (1.20–23)

Matthew repeatedly stops, stands like a guide, and tell us to pay
attention—pointing with one hand to some centuries-old-proph-
ecy, and with the other hand to Jesus as the fulfillment.

This was to **fulfill** what the Lord had spoken by the prophet, "Out of Egypt I called my son." (2.15)

Then was **fulfilled** what was spoken by the prophet Jeremiah: "A voice was heard in Ramah…" (2.17)

And he went and lived in a city called Nazareth, so that what was spoken by the prophets might be **fulfilled**, that he would be called a Nazarene. (2.23)

And leaving Nazareth he went and lived in Capernaum by the sea, in the territory of Zebulun and Naphtali, so that what was spoken by the prophet Isaiah might be **fulfilled**: "…the people dwelling in darkness have seen a great light…" (4.13–16)

This was to **fulfill** what was spoken by the prophet Isaiah: "He took our illnesses and bore our diseases." (8.17)

This was to **fulfill** what was spoken by the prophet Isaiah: "Behold, my servant whom I have chosen…" (12.17–21)

This was to **fulfill** what was spoken by the prophet: "I will open my mouth in parables…" (13.35)

This took place to **fulfill** what was spoken by the prophet, saying, "…Behold, your king is coming to you, humble, and mounted on a donkey…" (21.4–5)

"But all this has taken place that the Scriptures of the prophets might be **fulfilled**." (26.56)

Then was **fulfilled** what had been spoken by the prophet Jeremiah, saying, "And they took the thirty pieces of silver…" (27.9–10)

Isn't this why Jesus will say in his most famous sermon, "Do not think that I have come to abolish the Law or the Prophets; I have not come to abolish them but to **fulfill** them" (Matt 5.17)?

"Listen," Matthew is challenging us. Those promises and prophecies of God? They've been realized and put into effect. He was telling us the truth all along. This Jesus of Nazareth not only spoke as one who had authority, he repeatedly proved why *we* should hear his words and do them.

> Therefore we must pay much closer attention to what we have heard, lest we drift away from it. For since the message declared by angels proved to be reliable, and every transgression or disobedience received a just retribution, how shall we escape if we neglect such a great salvation? (Heb 2.1–3)

Fulfillment walked among us. He made promises and prophecies of his own. "He who has ears to hear, let him hear" (Luke 8.8).

# FRIDAY

## *Getting the Bible "Through" Me*

Deuteronomy 17 is a portion of Moses' farewell speech to Israel. In this chapter, Moses is encouraging the people to think about future kings who might come to reign over the nation.

> "When you come to the land that the LORD your God is giving you, and you possess it and dwell in it and then say, 'I will set a king over me, like all the nations that are around me,' you may indeed set a king over you whom the LORD your God will choose. One from among your brothers you shall set as king over you. You may not put a foreigner over you, who is not your brother. Only he must not acquire many horses for himself or cause the people to return to Egypt in order to acquire many horses, since the LORD has said to you, 'You shall never return that way again.' And he shall not acquire many wives for himself, lest his heart turn away, nor shall he acquire for himself excessive silver and gold." (Deut 17.14–17)

Notice the pitfalls that the future king (and all of us) must carefully avoid, "lest his heart turn away."

- **Pride:** "many horses for himself"
- **Sex:** "many wives for himself"
- **Possessions:** "excessive silver and gold for himself"

You may not be a king over ancient Israel, but the same pitfalls exist, even today. The same temptations can and *do* entice hearts into turning away from God. The divinely-prescribed safeguard against such a turning is worth noting.

> "And when he sits on the throne of his kingdom, he shall write for himself in a book a copy of this law, approved by the Levitical priests. And it shall be with him, and he shall read in it all the days of his life, that he may learn to fear the LORD his God by keeping all the words of this law and these statutes, and doing them, that his heart may not be lifted up above his brothers, and that he may not turn aside from the commandment, either to the right hand or to the left, so that he may continue long in his kingdom, he and his children, in Israel." (17.18–20)

**The most effective safeguard against your heart turning away from God is getting God's word into your heart.** The king was expected to write for himself a copy of God's law, keep it with him, and read it all the days of his life. To what practical effect?

- That he may learn to fear the Lord his God
- Keeping all the words of the law and statutes
- That his heart may not be lifted up above his brothers
- That he may not turn aside from the commandment

The real goal of Bible reading isn't to simply "get through" the Bible. The goal is get the Bible through me. Let's work on that today.

# SATURDAY

## *The Band Room of Your Body*

**Instruments**. There are different kinds of instruments—brass, stringed, woodwind, and percussion—designed and built "for" different purposes. Use a clarinet for percussion and you'll end up with splinters. You can't blow a guitar or pluck a tuba. Different instruments have been created "for" different purposes.

With that in mind, notice what the Holy Spirit communicates in Romans 6.12–13:

> Let not sin therefore reign in your mortal body, to make you obey its passions. Do not present your members to sin as instruments for unrighteousness, but present yourselves to God as those who have been brought from death to life, and your members to God as instruments for righteousness.

Your members—the members of *your* body—weren't created "for" unrighteousness any more than a flute was created "for" drumming. Think about that.

Your mind wasn't created "for" jealousy. Your heart wasn't created "for" idolatry. Your eyes weren't created "for" sexual immorality. Your ears weren't created "for" impurity. Your mouth wasn't created "for" gossip. Your hands weren't created "for" stealing. But present the members of your body "to" sin as instruments "for" unrighteousness and sin *will* reign in your body.

There's a better way. What if we actually harmonized our instruments with the original intentions of the Creator?

Your mind was created "for" worship. Your heart was created "for" joy. Your eyes were created "for" kindness. Your ears were created "for" goodness. Your mouth was created "for" love. Your hands were created "for" serving. Present the members of your body "to" God as instruments "for" righteousness? That's life, the way it was meant to be.

Violins don't play themselves. Trumpets don't sound on their own. They are just instruments—designed, built, presented, and used for a purpose.

Your body was also given to you for a purpose—God's purpose. Today you have the choice: in whose service will I use my instruments? Whose lead will I follow?

# WEEK TWO

## SUNDAY

### *Choose Your Shepherd Carefully*

We're much more familiar with Psalm 23—"The LORD is my shepherd; I shall not want"—than Psalm 49, a psalm of the sons of Korah. Psalm 49 is an honest look at "the path of those who have foolish confidence" (49.13), men and women who are treading paths of "iniquity" (49.5). They trust "in their wealth" (49.6), calling "lands by their own names" (49.11). They are people of "pomp" (49.12). While they live, they count themselves "blessed" (49.18). But here's the terrifying part: **"death shall be their shepherd"** (49.14).

What a stark contrast, a night-and-day difference laid before us as a fork in the road: the path of Psalm 23 vs. the path of Psalm 49.

### The Path of Psalm 23: "The LORD is my shepherd"

- He makes me lie down in green pastures
- He leads me beside still waters
- He restores my soul
- He leads me in paths of righteousness for his name's sake
- Even though I walk through the valley of the shadow of death, I will fear no evil
- My shepherd is with me
- His rod and his staff, they comfort me

**In the other direction, the Path of Psalm 49**

- I have confidence in myself
- I'm paving my own path
- I trust in my stuff
- I'm successful in the eyes of my peers
- I'm surrounded by pomp wherever I go
- I count myself blessed because of my accomplishments
- People know my name
- …but death *shall be my shepherd*

Man in his pomp yet without understanding is like the beasts that perish. (Psa 49.20)

Psalm 23 and Psalm 49. Two very different paths that end in very different places.

May we choose our shepherd carefully today.

# MONDAY

## *The God Who Has Been My Shepherd*

In Genesis 48, Jacob is a very old man—147 years old, to be exact (47.28). He was ill (48.1), and knew that the time was drawing near that he must die (47.29). In Genesis 48.15, this old man makes a remarkable statement as he's blessing the sons of Joseph.

"The God before whom my fathers Abraham and Isaac walked, **the God who has been my shepherd all my life long to this day...**"

That's a profound reality worth meditating upon today: the almighty Creator of the universe is willing to be the perfectly compassionate, gracious, protective shepherd of *my* life. If you know Jacob's story, you know that at times he had been a self-seeking, manipulative, stubborn "sheep," living up to the literal meaning of his name (*He cheats*) on more than one occasion.

And yet, the God of his fathers didn't misplace or abandon this wild sheep. God was willing to rescue, cleanse, and provide for him. It took Jacob longer than some to realize that fact. Running, wrestling, fearful confrontations, and dark nights of uncertainty were hurdles that had to be cleared. But when Jacob was willing to yield, submit, and embrace God as *his* God (33.20), he came to realize that the perfect shepherd had been there all along.

Not one of us knows exactly when our time on this earth will end. What we *can* know is that the gracious shepherd hasn't given up on us. Though we've wandered far from his perfect will for our lives, he is willing to rescue. Though we've wallowed in the mud and muck of selfish stubbornness, he is willing to cleanse. Though we bear the self-inflicted scrapes and scars of our own foolishness, the perfect shepherd is willing to heal and restore.

"The God who has been my shepherd all my life long to this day." I want to be able to confidently say those words at the end of my own time on this earth. Today is a good day to remind myself that it's possible, but only if I'm willing to yield, submit to, and embrace the God of Jacob as *my* God.

# TUESDAY

## *That Sort of Woman*

One of the Pharisees asked [Jesus] to eat with him, and he went into the Pharisee's house and reclined at table. And behold, a woman of the city, who was a sinner, when she learned that he was reclining at table in the Pharisee's house, brought an alabaster flask of ointment, and standing behind him at his feet, weeping, she began to wet his feet with her tears and wiped them with the hair of her head and kissed his feet and anointed them with the ointment. Now when the Pharisee who had invited him saw this, he said to himself, "If this man were a prophet, he would have known who and what sort of woman this is who is touching him, for she is a sinner." (Luke 7.36–39)

In fact, Jesus knew exactly "what sort of woman" she was.

In her brokenness and desperation, she was the sort of woman who was willing to enter a potentially hostile environment because a moment with Jesus would be worth more than the shame from those who would look down on her.

Bringing an alabaster flask of ointment, she was the sort of woman who was willing to make a sacrifice.

She had a reputation, clearly, but she was the sort of woman who was willing to humble herself. Perhaps, as she stood behind Jesus—at his feet—she whispered the words she had heard him say. "Blessed are the poor in spirit."

She was the sort of woman who was willing to weep over the mess she had made and her utter unworthiness to have even a second of his holy attention. "Blessed are those who mourn, for they shall be comforted."

She was the sort of woman who wanted to honor Jesus. Almost certainly she didn't have a house like *this* house that belonged to the Pharisee. But she did have her tears, the hair of her head, and a window of opportunity to kiss his feet and anoint him. "Blessed are the meek."

She was the sort of woman who had racked up a debt she could never repay. She was a woman of the city. A sinner. In that moment, Jesus knew exactly "what sort of woman" she was.

She was the sort of woman who loved him, the sort of woman who had faith in him, and as a result, she was the sort of woman who heard him say—to *her*—"Your sins are forgiven. Your faith has saved you; go in peace." She was the sort of woman who was able to leave that Pharisee's house a different sort of woman. Welcomed. Recognized. Valued. Redirected. With hope. Full of joy. At peace.

"Blessed are the pure in heart, for they shall see God." (Matt 5.8)

She did indeed. Be "that sort of woman" today.

# WEDNESDAY

## *Today's Resolve Shapes Tomorrow's Reality*

But Daniel resolved... (Dan 1.8)

He was forcibly removed from his homeland by Nebuchadnezzar, king of Babylon, and replanted in the heart of a pagan empire. He was one in a group of "youths without blemish, of good appearance and skillful in all wisdom, endowed with knowledge, understanding learning," judged "competent to stand" in Nebuchadnezzar's palace. He was to be given a three year reeducation in the literature and language of the Chaldeans—assigned a different diet, a different name, and a different trajectory for the rest of his captive life.

**"But Daniel resolved."** He remembered who (and whose) he was, resisting the pressure to conform. He refused to be defiled, respectfully but unashamedly requesting a distinctive path forward.

And Daniel was there until the first year of King Cyrus. (Dan 1.21)

It's easy to miss what we're being told in Daniel 1, but don't fly too quickly past that last verse. **"Daniel was there."** He had been taken captive as a youth in 605 BC. He was there, nineteen years later, when news of Jerusalem's destruction reached the palaces of Babylon. Daniel was there as kings proudly rose, were humbled, and fell. Over and over again, Daniel had the uncomfortable task of delivering unpopular news to unbelieving powers. He was there during an empire-wide prohibition on prayer. Overnight in a den of lions? Daniel was there. As mighty Babylon eroded and the Persians ascended, Daniel was there, a distinctive light in the darkness. Daniel was there when a bold messenger of out-of-season truths was needed. Kings came and went, empires rose and fell, but for more than 70 years, "Daniel was there."

That long and difficult journey had a beginning. A first step. Where did it start? With a "but," when Daniel, as a youth, resolved to live, no matter what, for God.

What about you? "I am resolved…" To do what? To *be* what? What will that resolve fuel within you? Will it be able to sustain you when life gets tough? Seventy years from now, where will that resolve have carried you?

"Daniel was there" because "Daniel resolved." Today's resolve shapes tomorrow's reality.

# THURSDAY

## *A Scene to Imagine When You Pray*

Many of us find prayer to be a life-giving, soul-enriching, ever-evolving challenge. At times, prayer seems to come naturally. At others, we feel like our wheels are spinning in a well-worn rut. If you're going through a "dry season" in your efforts to pray, here's something that has helped me: slowly read Revelation 4, close your eyes, and envision the words of your prayer echoing within that awesome scene.

Revelation 4 describes a throne in heaven. Someone is seated on that throne with the appearance of jasper and carnelian. Around the throne is a rainbow with the appearance of an emerald and twenty-four other thrones, with twenty-four elders seated on them. These elders are clothed in white garments with golden crowns on their heads. From the throne come flashes of lightning, rumblings, and peals of thunder.

There are seven torches of fire in front of the throne. Before the throne, there is a sea of glass, like crystal. Around the throne, on each side, are four living creatures, full of eyes in front and behind. One is like a lion. Another is like an ox. The next has the face of a man. The last is like an eagle in flight. Each of them has six wings. Day and night they say,

> "Holy, holy, holy, is the Lord God Almighty,
>    who was and is and is to come!"

They never stop.

"Holy, holy, holy, is the Lord God Almighty,
    who was and is and is to come!"

As they perpetually give glory and honor and thanks to the one seated on the throne, the twenty-four elders fall down before him, casting their crowns before his majesty, and continually worship, saying,

"Worthy are you, our Lord and God,
    to receive glory and honor and power,
for you created all things,
    and by your will they existed and were created."

Can you picture that incredible scene? Now realize that in the next chapter—Revelation 5—"the prayers of the saints" are described as incense in golden bowls that surround that throne. **That. Is. Extraordinary.**

Through the sacrifice and priesthood of Jesus, access has been granted for us to draw near to this throne with confidence (Heb 4.14–16). The invitation has been extended to cast all our anxieties before this throne, because its eternal occupant cares for us (1 Pet 5.6–7).

Before you pray again, slowly read Revelation 4, close your eyes, and envision your prayer being heard within the throne room of the Lord God Almighty.

# FRIDAY

### *The World's Greatest Empires, Like Utensils in His Hands*

A healthy dose of perspective from Jeremiah 51…

**Babylon.** "A destroyer of nations." The birthplace of wondrous architectural marvels. One of the most iconic empires in the history of the world. But in the grand scheme of things? "Babylon was a golden cup in the LORD's hand" (Jer 51.7).

**The Medes.** The next empire on the world stage. A destroyer from the north, humbler of mighty Babylon. But in the grand scheme of things? "You are my hammer," says the LORD (Jer 51.20).

That golden cup most certainly would have been something to behold, and that hammer undoubtedly left a mark on human history, but even the nicest cups come and go. The strongest hammers eventually break. And yet, one constant remains.

> It is he who made the earth by his power,
>> who established the world by his wisdom,
> and by his understanding stretched out the heavens. (Jer 51.15)

Our 21st century has its own "cups" and "hammers." We would do well to view them through the perspective-shaping lens of passages like Jeremiah 51. Let's recognize them for what they are. Dazzling, but temporary. Powerful, yet fragile. Definitely not ultimate. By no means eternal.

So let's not become so enamored with the sparkles of the "cups" or frustrated by the clanging of the "hammers" that we fail to recognize and honor the One who has used the world's greatest empires like everyday utensils to accomplish his purposes. It is he who made the earth. It is his wisdom that endures. It is his understanding that ultimately matters.

Therefore, let us be grateful for receiving a kingdom that cannot be shaken, and thus let us offer to God acceptable worship, with reverence and awe, for our God is a consuming fire. (Heb 12.28–29)

# SATURDAY

## *Refreshed to Refresh*

For I have derived much joy and comfort from your love, my brother, because the hearts of the saints have been refreshed through you. (Philemon 7)

Take a moment to think about what it feels like to be **refreshed**. A good night's sleep after a long and trying day. A cup of cold water in the shade after hours of work in the sun. A few days off after having your nose to the grindstone for months. Our bodies and minds need periodic refreshment.

So do our hearts—not the blood pumps in our chests, but our inner beings—the fount of our feelings and affections and determinations. That's one of the things that stood out about a first-century disciple in Colossae named Philemon. He was a source of refreshment to the hearts of the saints around him.

Notice that this wasn't just a personality trait or the side-effect of being a people-person.

I thank my God always when I remember you in my prayers, because I hear of your love and of the faith that you have toward the Lord Jesus and for all the saints... (4–5)

Philemon was a channel, not a reservoir. Philemon was a participant, not a spectator. Like a branch of a vine, he was drawing life, purpose, joy, comfort, hope, love, and peace from Christ and passing those blessings on to others. Even an apostle had "derived much joy and comfort" from Philemon's love (7) and was able to request in a difficult and awkward situation, "Refresh my heart in Christ" (20).

**Two things to think about today:**

First, if we're going to be similar sources of life, purpose, joy, comfort, hope, love, and peace to others, we need healthy *personal* connections to Jesus. We cannot share what we do not have. Let's drink deeply from the well of living water today in order to refresh ourselves and have something meaningful to pass on to others.

Second, like an ice-cold bottle of water in the desert, the refreshers are going to stand out (for the right reasons) in a season where many are spending their days and using their voices to grumble, groan, quarrel, gossip, backbite, slander, and tear down. That conduct may result in short-term attention, but it flows downhill into a dark reservoir of bitterness and ruin. Disciples of Jesus are to be known for better attitudes, actions, and reactions. We are transformed, renewed channels of blessing—loved, steadfast, immovable, abounding in the Lord's work to the Lord's glory.

All of which leads to this question: whose heart could use some refreshment in Christ today?

# WEEK THREE

## SUNDAY

*Three Seeds for Your Prayers This Week*

Take the time to meditate on three verses from **Psalm 56**—three seeds worth planting in your heart and integrating into your prayers this week. Three thousand years ago, David said *to* God and *of* God:

> When I am afraid,
>> I put my trust in you. (56.3)

God is greater than our fears and uncertainties. He is worthy of our trust. God is able to bear the weight of all our cares and anxieties. God is.

> You have kept count of my tossings;
>> put my tears in your bottle.
>> Are they not in your book? (56.8)

God knows the tossings and wrestlings of our hearts. God sees every one of our tears, and God cares.

> This I know,
>> that God is for me. (56.9)

God is, God cares, and God is *for* me. "Therefore," why wouldn't I say with David, "in God, whose word I praise, in God I trust" (56.4)?

Let's praise him this morning, trust him today, and use these three verses from Psalm 56 as life-giving seeds for our prayers this week.

# MONDAY

## *On Guard Against Being Undone*

Ahaziah was crowned king of Judah at twenty-two years old.

> His mother's name was Athaliah, the granddaughter of Omri. He also walked in the ways of the house of Ahab, for his mother was his counselor in doing wickedly. He did what was evil in the sight of the LORD, as the house of Ahab had done. For after the death of his father **they were his counselors, to his undoing.** (2 Chron 22.2–4)

A king of God's people, "undone" by the influence of the people around him.

We live in a noisy world full of "counselors" who are more than willing to tell you exactly what they think … and what *you* should think. All sorts of opinions, preferences, prejudices, and propaganda—mixed with a toxic swirl of unrighteousness and ungodliness—will take every ounce of the attention you're willing to yield this week. As a disciple of Jesus, don't allow these "counselors" to be your "undoing."

Don't let social media be the undoing of your love.

Don't let the pessimist be the undoing of your joy.

Don't let "breaking news" be the undoing of your peace.

Don't let traffic be the undoing of your patience.

Don't let that one rude person be the undoing of your kindness.

Don't let the ungratefulness of the few be the undoing of your goodness.

Don't let the fool with a YouTube channel be the undoing of your faithfulness.

Don't let the angry commenter who just likes to stir the pot be the undoing of your gentleness.

Don't let that person who has given into temptation, now inviting you to follow, be the undoing of your self-control.

You can only yield so much attention before access to your heart is granted. Listen with discernment. Weigh what you're hearing with divine wisdom. Seek first God's kingdom and righteousness. Set your mind on things above. Tune out the vain noise. Be serious about guarding your heart.

Our spirits were rightly lifted in worship yesterday. Don't allow anyone or anything to "undo" what matters most this week.

# TUESDAY

## *The Launching Point of a Terrible Trajectory*

In 1 Timothy 5, Paul uses three phrases to warn us away from a terrible trajectory.

1. In verse 6, he describes a "self-indulgent" woman who is "dead even while she lives."
2. In verse 11, he sounds the alarm that personal "passions" can "draw" us "away from Christ."
3. In verse 15, he laments the fact that "some have already strayed after Satan."

How does a disciple of Jesus—a man or woman who has been heaven-bound—"stray after Satan"? Just work your way back up that list above. We "stray after Satan" by being "drawn away" from Christ.

Each person is tempted when he is lured and enticed... (James 1:14a)

Lured and enticed by what?

...by his own desire... (James 1:14b)

...or, as Paul puts it in 1 Timothy 5, **self-indulgence**—the launching point of a terrible trajectory. Choosing self over God. Exalting self above others. Centering life on self. Setting aside what I know to be true in order to gratify myself. Indulging in the fleeting pleasures of sin at the expense of the ultimate reward.

...and sin when it is fully grown brings forth death. (James 1.15)

This is how a man or woman can be dead spiritually even as he or she is alive and well physically.

All of which means, we need to be self-aware today. More than that, we need to put our *selves* in their proper places. We need reminding that "our old self was crucified with Christ in order that the body of sin might be brought to nothing, so that we would no longer be enslaved to sin" (Rom 6.6). We've been given the opportunity to live as self*less* "sacrifices" today, "holy and acceptable to God," which is our spiritual worship (Rom 12.1).

Maybe that's the most succinct way of summarizing the whole thing: **Who am I going to worship today?** "All of self and none of Thee" is the path to slavery and death. "None of self and all of Thee" is the path to joyful freedom and life.

# WEDNESDAY

## *"I Am Doing a Work In Your Days"*

We're not the first to grapple with those big questions when life gets hard: Why is this happening? How long will it last? Where is God? More than 26 centuries ago, Habakkuk the prophet was confused.

> O LORD, how long shall I cry for help,
> and you will not hear?
> Or cry to you "Violence!"
> and you will not save?
> Why do you make me see iniquity,
> and why do you idly look at wrong?
> Destruction and violence are before me;
> strife and contention arise.
> So the law is paralyzed,
> and justice never goes forth.
> For the wicked surround the righteous;
> so justice goes forth perverted. (Hab 1.2–4)

Listen carefully to the LORD's response:

> "Look among the nations, and see;
> wonder and be astounded.
> For I am doing a work in your days
> that you would not believe if told." (Hab 1.5)

**"I am doing a work in your days."** That's a phrase worth thinking about today.

Habakkuk was frustrated. His perspective was clouded by swirling questions of How? Why? Where? And it was easy in that season to begin making assumptions about God. "Why can't he see what I can see so clearly? Has he checked out? Doesn't he care? Is he unable or unwilling to save?"

Habakkuk 1 reminds us that the Lord of heaven and earth was (and is) hearing just fine. He wasn't idly looking at wrong. His law wasn't paralyzed. Justice hadn't gone extinct. He hadn't forgotten his people or his promises. He was perfectly able to intervene. And he was "doing a work" in Habakkuk's days, even when the prophet couldn't see it.

We live in a different era, a different context, within the scope of a completely different (and better) covenant. But isn't that straightforward statement still worth meditating upon and carrying with us throughout the day? "I am doing a work in your days."

That work may not be what we expect. It probably isn't being carried out the way *we* would envision. It may be the polar opposite of our hopes and dreams; that was certainly true in Habakkuk's case. At times, we may find it hard to believe. We're not the first. But isn't the God of perfect providence still "doing a work" in our days? We may feel frustrated or confused or uncertain about where it's all going, but the Lord of heaven and earth continues to hear just fine. He isn't idly looking at wrong. His law isn't paralyzed. Justice hasn't gone extinct. He hasn't forgotten his people or his promises. He's continuing to weave a tapestry far more abundantly beautiful beyond all that we could ever imagine.

This morning's reading from Habakkuk 1 made me think of the much more familiar Romans 8.

> For in this hope we were saved. Now hope that is seen is not hope. For who hopes for what he sees? But if we hope for what we do not see, we wait for it with patience.

Likewise the Spirit helps us in our weakness. For we do not know what to pray for as we ought, but the Spirit himself intercedes for us with groanings too deep for words. And he who searches hearts knows what is the mind of the Spirit, because the Spirit intercedes for the saints according to the will of God. And we know that for those who love God all things work together for good, for those who are called according to his purpose. (8.24–28)

"I am doing a work in your days that you would not believe if told," and equipped with that perspective…

…we rejoice in our sufferings, knowing that suffering produces endurance, and endurance produces character, and character produces hope, and hope does not put us to shame, because God's love has been poured into our hearts through the Holy Spirit who has been given to us. (Rom 5.3–5)

# THURSDAY

## *A Good Day to Pray for Compassion*

And Jesus went throughout all the cities and villages, teaching in their synagogues and proclaiming the gospel of the kingdom and healing every disease and every affliction. When he saw the crowds, he had compassion for them, because they were harassed and helpless, like sheep without a shepherd. (Matt 9.35–36)

**Compassion.** Compassion is a sympathetic awareness of what others are experiencing and a willingness to do what you can to help. But compassion can be hard to "have" when we're...

...tired ... frustrated ... angry ... confused ... discouraged ... disillusioned ... running low on patience ... uncertain about the future ...

...and isn't that where a lot of us are? As a result, maybe the compassion gauge on the dashboard of our hearts is running dangerously low and the effects can be felt...

...at home ... in our marriages ... with our kids ... at work ... with our brothers and sisters in Christ ... in our attitude towards the needy ... the exhausted ... the hurting ... the grieving among us ...

...and the temperature of our spirits is running dangerously high with...

...the disagreeable ... the rude ... those on different sides of judgment calls ... those doing their best to make wise decisions for the good of the many ... those on the opposite end of the political spectrum ... those who have walked away ... those who have decided to look at us as the enemy.

When Jesus saw the harassed, helpless, hurting crowds, he had compassion for them. Amazing. But don't miss what he did next.

Then he said to his disciples, "The harvest is plentiful, but the laborers are few; therefore pray earnestly to the Lord of the harvest to send out laborers into his harvest." (Matt 9.37–38)

The harassed, helpless, and hurting are *everywhere*. Therefore pray. Pray earnestly. Pray for your heart. Pray for compassion, patience, and empathy, because it's awfully hard to share what you do not have, and the opportunities to share are everywhere. All around us.

If we prayed like that today and followed in the footsteps of Jesus, who knows what the Lord of the harvest might reap next?

# FRIDAY

### *How Would 1.1 of Your Book Begin?*

He was the greatest of all the people of the east.

7 sons. 3 daughters. 7,000 sheep. 3,000 camels. 500 yoke of oxen. 500 female donkeys. Very many servants.

And he lost it all in a single day.

> Then Job arose and tore his robe and shaved his head and fell on the ground and worshiped. And he said, "Naked I came from my mother's womb, and naked shall I return. The LORD gave, and the LORD has taken away; blessed be the name of the LORD." In all this Job did not sin or charge God with wrong. (Job 1.20–22)

How? How do you lose so much and respond with worship? Where do you find it within yourself to bless the LORD in the face of such devastation? What sort of anchor keeps you from knee-jerk sin in the midst of such a bitter storm?

In order to understand the "How?" in the wake of the disasters, we have to appreciate who Job was *before* the disasters.

> There was a man in the land of Uz whose name was Job, and that man was blameless and upright, one who feared God and turned away from evil. (Job 1.1)

It didn't take the loss of very many servants to get Job thinking about life the way it was meant to be. It didn't take the loss of thousands of livestock to motivate Job to walk the path of righteousness. It didn't take the loss of ten children to convince Job to slow down and build a relationship with God. The rain fell, the floods came, the winds blew and beat on Job to a near-unimaginable extent, but he did not fall. "In all this Job did not sin or charge God with wrong." Why? How? He had built his life on the rock before his greatest test began.

It makes me wonder, if there was a book of the Bible that bore my name, what would Chapter 1, Verse 1 say?

# SATURDAY

## *Unusual Kindness*

After we were brought safely through, we then learned that the island was called Malta. The native people showed us unusual kindness, for they kindled a fire and welcomed us all, because it had begun to rain and was cold. (Acts 28.1–2)

**Unusual**. The "unusual" is uncommon. The "unusual" is rare. The "unusual" makes people curious because it's peculiar. The "unusual" stands out like a sore thumb in the usual of the common.

Two-thousand years ago, Luke—the author of the New Testament *Acts of the Apostles*—was with Paul and many others who suffered a terrible shipwreck on a tiny island in the Mediterranean called Malta. The first thing Luke tells us about the people who lived on that island? They were "unusually kind."

What a great reminder and goal to adopt as we head into the weekend. To whom can you be "unusually kind" over the next few days?

The new neighbors? The grocery store cashier? The spouse you've been taking for granted? The elderly brother or sister in Christ at the nursing home? The young person who just moved into town to start college? The deacon who has served the local church for years behind the scenes? That grumpy person who was recently unkind to you? The new faces in your pew on Sunday morning?

Of all the people in all the world, the heaven-bound ought to be known for many "unusual" things. One of them? The showing of "unusual kindness."

> Be kind to one another, tenderhearted, forgiving one another, as God in Christ forgave you. (Eph 4.32)

# WEEK FOUR

## SUNDAY

### *Behold, Believe, Become*

The idols of the nations are silver and gold,
    the work of human hands.
They have mouths, but do not speak;
    they have eyes, but do not see;
they have ears, but do not hear,
    nor is there any breath in their mouths.
**Those who make them become like them,**
    **so do all who trust in them.** (Psa 135.15–18)

We become what we behold and believe.

The idols of the nations couldn't speak, see, or hear. They were the lifeless works of human hands—unable to consider, discern, or deliver. But human beings become what we behold and believe. Describing the man who would pray to the idol of his own making—"Deliver me, for you are my god!"—Isaiah laments:

> "They know not, nor do they discern, for he has shut their eyes, so that they cannot see, and their hearts, so that they cannot understand. No one considers, nor is there knowledge or discernment to say, 'Half of it I burned in the fire; I also baked bread on its coals; I roasted meat and have eaten. And shall I make the rest of it an abomination? Shall I fall down before a block of wood?' He feeds on ashes; a deluded heart has led him astray, and he cannot deliver himself…" (Isa 44.18–20)

Eyes that couldn't see, ears that couldn't hear, and hearts that didn't understand. But Isaiah wasn't talking about the blocks of wood. He was talking about people who slowly became what they beheld and believed.

Isn't that why the Holy Spirit calls us to "behold" some One, not some thing? Someone worthy of our belief and becoming?

> We all, with unveiled face, beholding the glory of the Lord, are being transformed into the same image from one degree of glory to another. For this comes from the Lord who is the Spirit. (2 Cor 3.18)

We become what we behold and believe, which ought to lead to some humble reflection and self-evaluation. What or who has my attention? With what am I filling my mind and fueling my heart? Is it true? Is he honorable? Is this just? Is that pure? Is she commendable? Are they worthy of praise?

We become what we behold and believe. The only question is whether we will be led deeper into delusion or further into glory.

# MONDAY

## *His Planting, His Work, For His Glory*

In Isaiah 60, as the LORD reveals what life would be like once the Redeemer had come to Zion (59.20), he describes his people as "the branch of my planting, the work of my hands, that I might be glorified" (60.21).

**His planting, his work, for his glory.** What a great lens through which to view myself, my life, and the world around me! How much more clearly could I see…

If I approached my job and work ethic as a branch of his planting, the work of his hands, that he might be glorified… Isn't that Colossians 3.23–24?

> Whatever you do, work heartily, as for the Lord and not for men, knowing that from the Lord you will receive the inheritance as your reward. You are serving the Lord Christ.

If I nourished and cherished my marriage as a branch of his planting, the work of his hands, that he might be glorified… Isn't that Ephesians 5.31–32?

> "Therefore a man shall leave his father and mother and hold fast to his wife, and the two shall become one flesh." This mystery is profound, and I am saying that it refers to Christ and the church.

If I approached parenthood as a branch of his planting, the work of his hands, that he might be glorified... Isn't that Ephesians 6.4?

> Fathers, do not provoke your children to anger, but bring them up in the discipline and instruction of the Lord.

If we remembered that the health and growth of the Lord's church is a branch of his planting, the work of his hands, that he might be glorified... Isn't that 1 Corinthians 3.5–7?

> What then is Apollos? What is Paul? Servants through whom you believed, as the Lord assigned to each. I planted, Apollos watered, but God gave the growth. So neither he who plants nor he who waters is anything, but only God who gives the growth.

If I treated the rest of my life—my time, opportunities, and responsibilities—as a branch of his planting, the work of his hands, that he might be glorified... Isn't that Ephesians 5.15–17?

> Look carefully then how you walk, not as unwise but as wise, making the best use of the time, because the days are evil. Therefore do not be foolish, but understand what the will of the Lord is.

**His planting, his work, for his glory.** How much more clearly could I see if I viewed the world through that lens?

> You are not your own, for you were bought with a price. So glorify God in your body. (1 Cor 6.19–20)

Bearing fruit as a branch of God's planting, the ongoing work of his hands, that he might be glorified. That's life the way it was meant to be.

# TUESDAY

*Knowing All That Would Happen to Him...*

When Jesus had spoken these words, he went out with his disciples across the brook Kidron, where there was a garden, which he and his disciples entered. Now Judas, who betrayed him, also knew the place, for Jesus often met there with his disciples. So Judas, having procured a band of soldiers and some officers from the chief priests and the Pharisees, went there with lanterns and torches and weapons. **Then Jesus, knowing all that would happen to him**, came forward and said to them, "Whom do you seek?" They answered him, "Jesus of Nazareth." Jesus said to them, "I am he." (John 18.1–5)

## Knowing all that would happen to him...

...Judas' betrayal, the arrest, the disciples' abandonment, the trials, the false witnesses, Peter's denial, the slaps, the mocking, the scourging, the long cross-bearing walk to Golgotha, the crucifixion, the weight of the sins of the world...

**...Jesus came forward.** How? Listen to what he had said earlier that same night.

"I am in the Father and the Father is in me." (14.10)

"I do as the Father has commanded me, so that the world may know that I love the Father." (14.31)

"I have kept my Father's commandments and abide in his love." (15.10)

"I am not alone, for the Father is with me." (16.32)

Not one of us knows how this week will unfold and what lies around the next bend of our own path. But if these truths served as sufficient fuel for Jesus—knowing all that would happen to him—can't they serve as a source of present help and courage and peace to us? If these truths could support the weight of knowing all that would happen to him over the next few hours, can't they continue to bear the weight of whatever comes my way this week? If we made those truths personal…

"I am in the Father and the Father is in me."

"I do as the Father has commanded me, so that the world may know that I love the Father."

"I have kept my Father's commandments and abide in his love."

"I am not alone, for the Father is with me."

…couldn't we walk in the light of Jesus' promise: "Peace I leave with you; my peace I give to you" (John 14.27)?

If knowing all that would happen to him didn't rob Jesus of his peace, isn't his lead worth following by faith this week?

# WEDNESDAY

*Blessed Beyond Measure, But Miserable*

"I can't even list all the amazing blessings, but they're trash to me as long as I don't have..."

What an ugly, shortsighted, self-centered attitude. In the early chapters of the Old Testament book of *Esther*, Haman the Agagite has risen to prominence in Persia, set by King Ahasuerus above all other officials. "And all the king's servants who were at the king's gate bowed down and paid homage to Haman" (3.2) ... all except a Jewish man named Mordecai. The "slight" fills Haman with such fury that he devises a plan to destroy every Jew in the kingdom.

How does a human heart sink to such darkness?

In Esther 5, Haman has enjoyed a feast with the king arranged by Queen Esther herself. He's even been personally invited to *another* feast with the royal pair tomorrow! He leaves joyful and glad of heart, "but when Haman saw Mordecai in the king's gate, that he neither rose nor trembled before him, he was filled with wrath" (5.9).

How does a human heart become so self-centered?

When Haman gets home, he can't wait to tell his wife and friends all about what he has enjoyed: the splendor of his riches, all the promotions with which the king has honored him, how he has advanced beyond every other official. "Even Queen Esther let no one but me come with the king to the feast she prepared. And tomorrow also I am invited by her together with the king. Yet all this is worth nothing to me, so long as I see Mordecai the Jew sitting at the king's gate" (5.10–13).

Blessed beyond measure, yet miserably fixated on the most trivial of things. "All this is worth nothing, so long as…" What an ugly, shortsighted attitude.

But that got me thinking. I see it, plain as day, in Haman. Do I suffer from a similar blind spot? The God and Father of my Lord Jesus has blessed me in Christ with every spiritual blessing in the heavenly places (Eph 1.3). The Son of God died for me. By grace I've been granted access to confidently draw near to the throne of the universe's Lord.

"I can't even list all the amazing blessings, but I don't have…"

"God has forgiven me over and over a debt I could never repay in 10,000 lifetimes, but you don't realize what that guy over there did to me…"

"The Holy Spirit bears witness that I'm a child of God, a fellow heir with Christ, but she has … and I've always wanted … so I can't even look at her without feeling resentful and bitter."

"I'm heaven-bound, but I've never been able to … and I'm going to be upset with God if he doesn't…"

Really? Isn't that the root ugliness we can so easily spot in Haman? Blessed beyond measure, but miserably fixated on the most trivial of things. Maybe looking through that lens will help us remember the call of Hebrews 13.5 today.

> Keep your life free from love of money, and be content with what you have, for [God] has said, "I will never leave you nor forsake you."

Is he enough? He is indeed, but sometimes we struggle to see (and believe) it.

# THURSDAY

## *Stable, Steadfast, Not Shifting*

Stable, steadfast, and not shifting—three characteristics to think about today.

> And you, who once were alienated and hostile in mind, doing evil deeds, he has now reconciled in his body of flesh by his death, in order to present you holy and blameless and above reproach before him, if indeed you continue in the faith, **stable** and **steadfast, not shifting** from the hope of the gospel that you heard, which has been proclaimed in all creation under heaven, and of which I, Paul, became a minister. (Col 1.21–23)

Stable, steadfast, and not shifting—that's what we're called to be as disciples of Jesus. But notice the foundation of the blessings. Appreciate the source of the strength. It's not me; it doesn't come as a result of me getting my act together. It's not my circumstances; it doesn't depend upon everything around me being exactly as I'd like it.

The foundation is "the faith." The fuel is "the hope of the gospel." And if I walk in "the faith," building my life on "the hope of the gospel," what I begin to experience and enjoy is…

**Stability.** I am established. Founded. I know who I am because I know whose I am.

**Steadfastness.** I am settled. At peace. In Christ alone my hope is found; he is my light, my strength, my song.

**Not shifting**. I am grounded, not tossed to and fro or carried about by the winds around me. The cornerstone of my life is embedded in solid ground, firm through the fiercest drought and storm.

This is the hope of the gospel which has been proclaimed throughout all creation for 2,000 years. And it begs the question: are you stable today? Steadfast? Not shifting? If not, what's missing? My guess is, it's right there in Colossians 1.

# FRIDAY

## *Tested, That We Might Know*

The children of Israel were on the doorstep. Forty years' worth of wilderness-wandering was behind them. The Promised Land was before them. In Deuteronomy 8, Moses—their aged leader—was offering his final reminders.

> "The whole commandment that I command you today you shall be careful to do, that you may live and multiply, and go in and possess the land that the LORD swore to give to your fathers. And you shall remember the whole way that the LORD your God has led you these forty years in the wilderness…"

"Remember the whole way…" The **way** the LORD had led these people was significant. So in what "way" had he led them?

> "…that he might humble you, testing you to know what was in your heart, whether you would keep his commandments or not. And he humbled you and let you hunger and fed you with manna, which you did not know, nor did your fathers know, that he might make you know that man does not live by bread alone, but man lives by every word that comes from the mouth of the LORD."

These people had been tested by God. They had been made to wander. They had experienced hunger and thirst. They had been fed strange food and led to drink water from rocks. But notice the **reasons** for the testing:

- That he might humble you
- That he might know what was in your heart
- That he might make you know that life comes from his words

"Your clothing did not wear out on you and your foot did not swell these forty years. Know then in your heart that, as a man disciplines his son, the LORD your God disciplines you. So you shall keep the commandments of the LORD your God by walking in his ways and by fearing him."

Now, with forty years' worth of wilderness-wandering behind them, Moses can look them in the eyes and say, **"Know then in your heart..."**

There's no doubt in my mind that some who will read these words today are in the midst of truly trying times. For some, the "Why?" is murky, the "How?" is foggy, and the "When?" is unknown. What *is* known is fear and worry and struggle and darkness.

If that sounds familiar, I hope this passage from the ancient book of Deuteronomy shines like a ray of light for you today. Tests are hard. Tests humble us. They challenge our faith and stretch our submission. But *through* the tests, perhaps we come to know what we did not know before. *Through* the tests, maybe we begin to appreciate what we took for granted for a very long time.

God kept a couple million Israelites alive in the wilderness, testing them, that he might **make them know**. Man does not live by bread alone, but by every word that comes from the mouth of God. And on the back end of those tests? There was knowledge to pass on, experience to share, wisdom to model, life to be enjoyed, and praise to be offered.

**"Know then in *your* heart..."**

# SATURDAY

## *A Holy Destroyer*

The reason Jesus came is…

You can use the Bible to fill in that blank with a variety of answers. The reason provided in 1 John 3.8 is worth thinking about today:

> The reason the Son of God appeared was to destroy the works of the devil.

**Our Savior and King is a holy Destroyer.** Consider just 1 John 3 as Exhibit-A.

**Jesus destroys *alienation* from God.** "See what kind of love the Father has given to us, that we should be called children of God; and so we are." (3.1)

**Jesus destroys *despair* over the future.** "Beloved, we are God's children now, and what we will be has not yet appeared; but we know that when he appears we shall be like him, because we shall see him as he is." (3.2)

**Jesus destroys *impurity*.** "Everyone who thus hopes in him purifies himself as he is pure." (3.3)

**Jesus destroys *sin*.** "You know that he appeared in order to take away sins, and in him there is no sin." (3.5)

**Jesus destroys *slavery*.** "No one who abides in him keeps on sinning." (3.6)

**Jesus destroys *selfishness*.** "By this we know love, that he laid down his life for us, and we ought to lay down our lives for the brothers." (3.16)

**Jesus destroys *hypocrisy*.** "Little children, let us not love in word or talk but in deed and in truth." (3.18)

**Jesus destroys *guilt*.** "By this we shall know that we are of the truth and reassure our heart before him; for whenever our heart condemns us, God is greater than our heart, and he knows everything." (3.19–20)

> The reason the Son of God appeared was to destroy the works of the devil.

> Don't allow the devil to reconstruct in your life what Jesus came to destroy.

# WEEK FIVE

## SUNDAY

### *Are You Walking Through a Museum or Looking in a Mirror?*

Psalm 106 is a look back at some sad moments in Israel's history. As we read it, we might naturally feel as if we're being led through the long hallway of a museum. Picture after picture, scene after scene depicts the shortcomings and failures of other people.

- In Exodus 14, Israel resisted being shaped by God's wondrous works and steadfast love (106.7–12)
- In Numbers 11, these descendants of Abraham allowed unrestrained cravings to override their willingness to wait for God's counsel (106.13–15)
- In Numbers 16, Korah, Dathan, and Abiram led many into rebellion out of jealousy and selfish ambition (106.16–18)
- In Exodus 32, Israel exchanged the glory of God for a golden calf they could make (106.19–23)
- In Numbers 14, they didn't believe God's promises and refused to follow his lead (106.24–27)
- In Numbers 25, a great many "yoked" themselves to blatant immorality (106.28–31)
- In Numbers 20, the people complained in the face of God's faithfulness (106.32–33)
- In the opening chapters of Judges, Israel settled for half-measures and compromised standards (106.34–39)

- Throughout the era of the judges, generation after generation took God's deliverance for granted (106.40–43)

There's a lot of "they" and "them" throughout this ancient poem, so it's easy to treat Psalm 106 like a long walk through the dark, dusty wing of a museum. Spend a few minutes passing through, read the captions, shake your head at the foolishness of people who lived a long time ago, and move on to something else.

But to treat Psalm 106 as a museum gallery of the past is to miss the point. It's not just "they" and "them," it's "we" and "us."

Both **we** and our fathers have sinned;
**we** have committed iniquity; **we** have done wickedness. (106.6)

Save **us**, O Lord our God... (106.47)

In fact, it hits even closer to home than "we" and "us." It's "me."

Remember **me**, O Lord, when you show favor to your people;
help **me** when you save them... (106.4)

Here's a valuable lesson for us, even thousands of years later. Don't treat God's word like a museum. People easily walk through museums, observe, and leave, unchanged. It was nothing more than "they" and "them."

When you open the Bible, treat it like a mirror (James 1.22–25). We look in mirrors to study, learn, and be transformed. "They" becomes "we," and "we" ultimately becomes "me." That's why a 3,000-year-old psalm is still worth reading:

- **I** need to be shaped by his wondrous works and steadfast love
- **I** must guard against allowing unrestrained cravings to override **my** willingness to wait for his counsel
- **I** am called to act from a heart of humility and kindness

- I must resist the temptation to seek anything or anyone above God and his glory
- I must choose to trust his promises and follow his lead
- I will present **my** body as a living sacrifice, holy and acceptable to God
- I will rejoice and express thanksgiving for his faithfulness and wisdom
- I will respect his authority and express **my** love by keeping his commandments
- I will appreciate the riches of his kindness and patience and grace, understanding that they are meant to lead **me** to repentance

God is still good (106.1). His steadfast love continues to endure forever (106.1). This God of "mighty deeds" (106.2) continues to bless those who observe justice and do righteousness (106.3). He remembers and helps his people (106.4–5). He is worthy of your praise and my praise (106.1), even today.

All of that begins to become clear when we look in the mirror.

# MONDAY

## *God's Book, Your Heart*

"I have found the Book of the Law in the house of the LORD."
(2 Kings 22.8)

How dark must life have been in Judah for the high priest to have
to notify the king's secretary that God's Book had been found?
And of all places, in the temple of the LORD? How had it been lost
in the first place?

> Then Shaphan the secretary told the king, "Hilkiah the priest has
> given me a book." And Shaphan read it before the king. (2 Kings
> 22.10)

How many of God's commandments did King Josiah hear—
at that reading—for the first time? In what ways had the temple
of the LORD been neglected during Josiah's reign? How much of
God's covenant with Israel had been completely forgotten by his
forefathers?

> When the king heard the words of the Book of the Law, he tore
> his clothes. (2 Kings 22.11)

Lost Book. Lost people. Lost king. But notice the connection
God draws between his Book and Josiah's heart.

> "Thus says the LORD, the God of Israel: Regarding the words that
> you have heard, because your heart was penitent, and you hum-

bled yourself before the LORD, when you heard how I spoke…"
(2 Kings 22.18–19)

Think about that. Long ago, God had preserved words in a Book. A time came in young Josiah's life when he personally heard those words read. And the reading of those ancient words had a profound impact on his heart.

Can't the same be true thousands of years later? Isn't this how our Creator continues to work? The words of the LORD (now fully revealed) can still be found in God's Book. Hearts can still be touched and transformed by the words in that Book. Men and women are still expected to humble themselves before God when they hear how he has spoken in his Book. A life-giving connection continues to exist between God's Book and human hearts.

Those are good reasons to spend time reading the Bible today. May its living influence not be "lost" in minivan backseats, on dusty shelves, and empty pews this week.

# TUESDAY

## *The Bridge Between My Response and His Return*

I give thanks to my God always for you because of the grace of God that was given you in Christ Jesus, that in every way you were enriched in him in all speech and all knowledge—even as the testimony about Christ was confirmed among you—so that you are not lacking in any gift, as you wait for the revealing of our Lord Jesus Christ, who will sustain you to the end, guiltless in the day of our Lord Jesus Christ. God is faithful, by whom you were called into the fellowship of his Son, Jesus Christ our Lord. (1 Cor 1.4–9)

**Called** into fellowship with God and **waiting** for the revealing of our Lord Jesus Christ. That's where we find ourselves in human history. *Called* and *waiting.*

Today, I'm thankful for the word in the middle that bridges the gap between my response to the gospel and Jesus' return. *Sustained.*

…as you wait for the revealing of our Lord Jesus Christ, **who will sustain you to the end**… (1 Cor 1.7–8)

*Sustained.* To *sustain* is to give support, to supply, or to keep up. Think about that.

Jesus died for our sins in accordance with the Scriptures. He has been triumphantly raised from the dead, the firstfruits of those who have fallen asleep. Ever since his ascension, his disciples have been waiting for the revealing of their Lord…

...but not waiting on their own. To this day, we are not waiting in our own strength, goodness, or wisdom. The face of God's grace, the friend for whom we wait, sustains us. Today, on an ordinary Tuesday, we wait for his revealing. And for as long as we have to wait, we are sustained. Till the end, his brothers and sisters will be sustained. Even in death, the faithful—now resting from their labors—are sustained.

Think about that. As you read and meditate on the Scriptures this week, you are being sustained. As you pray this week, you are being sustained. As you worship, you are being sustained.

"I am the vine; you are the branches. Whoever abides in me and I in him, he it is that bears much fruit, for apart from me you can do nothing." (John 15.5)

As branches wait for the rain, we wait *for* him, *in* him. God is faithful. He always has been. He will be. "To the end."

# WEDNESDAY

## *There's No Such Thing as a Secret Sin*

"For you did it secretly, but…" (2 Sam 12.12)

"Thus says the LORD" to David through Nathan the prophet. Why? Throughout 2 Samuel 11, David had acted secretly.

- He secretly looked at a woman named Bathsheba with lustful intent
- He secretly inquired about her identity
- He secretly took her and committed adultery
- He secretly sent for her husband Uriah after hearing of her pregnancy
- He secretly got Uriah drunk to complete the cover-up
- He secretly engineered Uriah's murder
- He secretly believed that with Uriah dead, he could marry Bathsheba, have the child, and move on, leaving his dark closet full of secrets … secret

The fundamental flaw in David's plan? There's really no such thing as a secret sin. "For you did it secretly, but…" God saw. God knew. "The thing that David had done (in secret) displeased the LORD" (1 Sam 11.27).

Ironically enough, it's David that God used to communicate to all people of all time:

If I say, "Surely the darkness shall cover me,
and the light about me be night,"
even the darkness is not dark to you;
the night is bright as the day,
for darkness is as light with you. (Psa 139.11–12)

In an era of "anonymous" apps, "disappearing" photos, "incognito" browsers, "no-strings-attached" hookups, and destinations that boldly advertise "What happens here stays here," let's remember … there's no such thing as secret sin. Our Creator "delights" when "truth" fills "the inward being" (Psa 51.6). So let's pray today with David, "teach me wisdom in the secret heart." Let's be honest with ourselves and, most importantly, with God.

# THURSDAY

*When You're Given a Front Row Seat to Suffering...*

Now it happened that as he was praying alone... (Luke 9.18)

I rented a small truck last night to move a refrigerator. If I didn't want to pay $8 per gallon, I was expected to return the truck with a full tank. As I swiped my card at the gas pump and started to reach for the same nozzle I always reach for, (thankfully) a light bulb went off in my head. Unleaded or diesel? There's a big difference between the engine in that moving truck and the engine in my Toyota Camry.

An opportunity of a different sort presented itself to all of us this morning: a new day with more time to open our God-given hearts to a world of possibilities, and what we pump into those hearts matters more than most of us probably realize.

If you're like me, it's way too easy to spend the morning "fueling up" on mostly meaningless, empty, earthbound stuff... sports scores, political news, overnight Instagram photos, trends on Twitter, the endless scroll of the Facebook feed...

...and then the phone rings, or the text arrives, or the email lands, or someone slows you down with tears in their eyes and you've suddenly been given a front row seat to a real need or heartache or doubt or fear...

...the diagnosis is cancer. There's been a miscarriage. The life of a loved one was tragically cut short. Infidelity is suspected. A prodigal child has wandered further away. The job was lost. The grief is getting heavier. The tears won't stop. The loneliness is nearly unbearable...

...and the day hasn't begun like I thought it would. I'm unexpectedly entrusted with a sacred opportunity to help bear a heavy burden. **But what do I have to offer in that moment?** What can I pour out? Is there anything fresh on my heart of more significance than last night's college basketball scores and the latest stock market projections? What strength has the celebrity gossip and the funny cat meme provided me?

The gospels are full of brief glimpses into what Jesus did with "down time." In desolate places. Early in the morning. Late at night. Before the crowds came knocking at the door.

"Now it happened that as he was praying alone..."

Life in this post-Genesis 3 world continues to happen, sometimes in ways that break our hearts. Am I making the most of my peaceful time in between the storms? When the darkness comes close enough to feel, do I have fuel to shine? When the earth quakes beneath my feet, am I grounded in God's wisdom and equipped to share eternal perspective with others? When sorrows like sea-billows roll, do I know where the anchor is? Have I been following in his holy footsteps—praying alone, meditating on God-breathed words, drinking deeply from life-giving fountains—so that no matter what is going on around me, I can still hear his voice? "It is I; do not be afraid."

Is today a good day for you so far? I hope it is. So let's think ahead. When the phone rings, or the text arrives, or the email lands, or someone stops us with tears in their eyes and we suddenly have a front row seat to suffering and doubt, will we have so recently walked with Jesus that it feels natural to stand in the gap and connect those trembling hands of the hurting to his?

# FRIDAY

## *The Difference Between Dying in the Wilderness and Inheriting the Promised Land*

The conclusion of Joshua 11 very matter-of-factly documents:

> And Joshua came at that time and cut off the Anakim from the hill country, from Hebron, from Debir, from Anab, and from all the hill country of Judah, and from all the hill country of Israel. Joshua devoted them to destruction with their cities. There was none of the Anakim left in the land of the people of Israel. Only in Gaza, in Gath, and in Ashdod did some remain. So Joshua took the whole land, according to all that the LORD had spoken to Moses. And Joshua gave it for an inheritance to Israel according to their tribal allotments. And the land had rest from war. (Josh 11.21–23)

Joshua and the people of his generation did what their parents' generation said could not be done. Remember?

> "We came to the land to which you sent us. It flows with milk and honey, and this is its fruit. However, the people who dwell in the land are strong, and the cities are fortified and very large. And besides, we saw the descendants of Anak there. The Amalekites dwell in the land of the Negeb. The Hittites, the Jebusites, and the Amorites dwell in the hill country. And the Canaanites dwell by the sea, and along the Jordan ... **We are not able to go up against the people, for they are stronger than we are.**" (Num 13.27–29, 31)

Both generations were encouraged to believe the same promise:

"The LORD is with us; do not fear them." (Num 14.9)

"Be strong and courageous. Do not be frightened, and do not be dismayed, for the LORD your God is with you wherever you go." (Josh 1.9)

One generation refused to believe; they grumbled against Moses and talked about going back to Egypt (Num 14.14). The next generation believed; they marched and fought and conquered. And in doing so, they *did* precisely what their parents' generation said could not be done. **It all depended upon faith (or lack thereof) in the promises of God.**

Which begs the question: of which generation am I figuratively a part? The generation that marched with Moses but failed to believe? Or the generation that marched with Joshua and believed? The answer to that question could be the difference between dying in the wilderness and inheriting the Promised Land.

# SATURDAY

## *The Priest Who Never Dies*

Aaron died there on the top of the mountain... And when all the congregation saw that Aaron had perished, all the house of Israel wept for Aaron thirty days. (Num 20.28–29)

He had served as the first high priest of Israel—a mere mortal, appointed to intercede between the people and the LORD. Now, Aaron was dead, and the nation wept for a month.

This makes Jesus the guarantor of a better covenant. (Heb 7.22)

What? How? Why, centuries later, would the writer of *The Letter to the Hebrews* say such a thing? Listen:

The former priests were many in number, because they were prevented by death from continuing in office, but [Jesus] holds his priesthood permanently, because he continues forever. Consequently, he is able to save to the uttermost those who draw near to God through him, since he always lives to make intercession for them. (Heb 7.23–25)

Aaron died. Generations of priests after him lived and served and died. High priest after high priest was prevented by death from continuing in office.

But Jesus lives. Always. Jesus holds—in the present tense—his priesthood. Permanently. His work continues to this day without disruption. He serves as high priest at this very moment, willing and able to intercede for those who draw near to God through him.

"We have such a high priest." Meditate on that incredible phrase today. The One who mediates on our behalf "has no need, like those high priests, to offer sacrifices daily, first for his own sins and then for those of the people, since he did this once for all when he offered up himself" (7.27). Jesus is the sacrificial lamb. Jesus is the resurrected priest. Jesus is the living, permanent intercessor and Christians have been given access to the throne of the universe, in his name.

The next time you bow your head and lift your heart in prayer, take a silent, reflective moment to appreciate how this makes Jesus the guarantor of a better covenant, then thank your Father in heaven that his Son always lives to make intercession for you.

# WEEK SIX

## SUNDAY

### *Don't Forget, We Know Where the River Ends*

In Psalm 73, Asaph is struggling with some seriously shortsighted perspective.

> Truly God is good to Israel, to those who are pure in heart. But as for me, my feet had almost stumbled, my steps had nearly slipped. For I was envious of the arrogant when I saw the prosperity of the wicked. (73.1–3)

The more Asaph sees, the more it seems like the wicked are enjoying "the good life":

> No pangs until death. Well-fed, healthy bodies. Not the same troubles as others. They wear pride like a necklace. Violence covers them as a garment, but they seem to always get away with it. Their hearts overflow with follies. They scoff and speak with malice. Arrogant threats of oppression. Mouths set against the heavens. Tongues strutting through the earth. Always at ease, increasing in riches, and free from the consequences of their wicked behavior.

Asaph's question: *Why?* Why does it seem like the wicked are prospering while the righteous are suffering? Are the holy keeping their hearts pure in vain? Have we washed our hands in innocence for nothing (73.13–15)?

But then Asaph remembers. **We've been told where the river ends**.

When I thought how to understand this, it seemed to me a wearisome task, until I went into the sanctuary of God; then I discerned their end. (73.16–17)

We might not ever be able to answer some of the biggest "Why?" questions during our brief time under the sun. Some bends in the river of life will continue to perplex. Rapids will continue to roar and the righteous, at times, will be caught in the undercurrents.

But God has provided perspective for those who are willing to hear, remember, and trust. The "end" *can* (and should) be discerned. All streams, rapids, and rivers eventually lead to his holy and awesome throne of righteous judgment. And at that point, will the wicked be in an enviable position? Not in the slightest.

Maybe you're struggling to keep your perspective lenses straight and clear today. If so, let the message of Psalm 73 sink in. Even *if* you don't know **why** and exactly **where** the river of life bends, but you know where it *ends*, isn't that what matters most? If you've been shown how to save yourself, your loved ones, and anyone else who is willing to submit to the Creator, don't you have what you need to live life well? And if your Savior and Friend is with you every bump and bend of the way, isn't that enough?

You hold my right hand. You guide me with your counsel, and afterward you will receive me to glory. Whom have I in heaven but you? And there is nothing on earth that I desire besides you. My flesh and my heart may fail, but God is the strength of my heart and my portion forever. (73.23–26)

Come what may, we know where the river ends.

# MONDAY

## *Sometimes, the Most Faithful Thing We Can Do Is Wait*

In 1 Samuel 13, the dreaded Philistines had mustered to fight with Israel. Thirty thousand chariots. Six thousand horsemen. Troops like the sand on the seashore in multitude.

Saul had been Israel's first king for two years. His people were hiding in caves, holes, tombs, and cisterns. Some had already fled across the Jordan. "All the people followed him trembling."

> [Saul] waited seven days, the time appointed by Samuel. But Samuel did not come to Gilgal, and the people were scattering from him. So Saul said, "Bring the burnt offering here to me, and the peace offerings." And he offered the burnt offering. As soon as he had finished offering the burnt offering, behold, Samuel came. And Saul went out to meet him and greet him. Samuel said, "What have you done?" (1 Sam 13.8–11)

**Sometimes, the most faithful thing we can do is wait.** Wait on the Lord. Trust his timing. Rely on his promises. Saul didn't.

> "When I saw that the people were scattering from me, and that you did not come within the days appointed, and that the Philistines had mustered at Michmash, I said, 'Now the Philistines will come down against me at Gilgal, and I have not sought the favor of the LORD.' So I forced myself, and offered the burnt offering." (1 Sam 13.11–12)

He felt control slipping away. He didn't understand why Samuel hadn't already arrived. He saw a powerful enemy gathering to pounce. He knew he was hopelessly outnumbered. And he reasoned, "My best choice is to *force* myself to overstep God's instructions. Take control back. Go ahead, do what needs to be done, and worry about the consequences later."

And Samuel said to Saul, "You have done foolishly." (1 Sam 13.13)

Many today live with the motto, "Better to ask forgiveness than permission." But if 1 Samuel 13 teaches us anything, surely it teaches us this: sometimes, the most faithful thing we can do is wait.

**As a new God-given week unfolds, we are waiting.**

The creation **waits** with eager longing (Rom 1.19). We ourselves groan inwardly as we **wait** eagerly for adoption as sons, the redemption of our bodies (Rom 1.23). We are **waiting** for our blessed hope, the appearing of the glory of our great God and Savior Jesus Christ (Titus 2.13). Through the Spirit, by faith, we eagerly **wait** for the hope of righteousness (Gal 5.5). According to his promise, we are **waiting** for new heavens and a new earth in which righteousness dwells (2 Pet 3.13).

Therefore, beloved, since you are waiting for these, be diligent to be found by him without spot or blemish, and at peace. (2 Pet 3.14)

That's a better motto to live by this week. Despite fears, obstacles, worries, disappointments, heartaches, and even your own pride, wait on the Lord. Trust his timing. Rely on his promises. "Keep yourselves in the love of God, waiting for the mercy of our Lord Jesus Christ that leads to eternal life" (Jude 21).

# TUESDAY

## *Known to Everyone ... For What?*

Let your reasonableness be known to everyone. The Lord is at hand. (Phil 4.5)

**Reasonableness.** Someone who is "reasonable" can be reasoned *with*. They recognize and are willing to adapt to a standard outside themselves. The reasonable person isn't extreme or excessive. He is steady. She is fair. Quick to hear, slow to speak, slow to anger. Calm. Composed. In control. Gentle, which is why the *New American Standard* translates Philippians 4.5 as "Let your gentle spirit be known to all men."

The reasonable person thinks before she speaks. He considers before he comments. She is discreet in what she shares. He is careful with his tone. She is willing to overlook a slight. He is mature enough to suffer wrong without returning wrong. In times of difficulty or chaos, reasonable people are looked to and depended upon for their sound judgment. Why? A reputation of stability has been formed, one interaction and impression after another.

Let your reasonableness be known to everyone...

It's never been easier (for good or ill) to make an impression on people. Spend time interacting on social media and some will believe they have come to "know" you. They may never actually meet you in the flesh, but an impression *of* you has already been made.

Which leads us to the question: **For what am I known?** Online? In the workplace? Among the congregation? At home?

Rash words? A quick temper? Pouting? Careless sharing? Gossip? Lying? Complaining? Discontentment? Rivalry? Provocation? Bitterness? Hatred? Prejudice? Abuse? Fits of anger? Recklessness? Retaliation? Escalation?

We don't have to wonder what disciples of Jesus are expected to be known for. By the Lord. Who is at hand.

Let your reasonableness be known to everyone...

But here's the tricky thing: in order to be known for our reasonableness, **we have to act reasonably**. If we are to build the reputation of being gentle, we have to actually live and interact with gentle spirits.

So what do you want to be known by everyone for? Impressions will be made today. Your reputation is perpetually under construction. Build wisely.

# WEDNESDAY

*Ancient Trash Talk and the Ever-Relevant Answer*

The inhabitants of Jerusalem found themselves at a crossroads in Isaiah 36. To whom were they going to listen?

From inside the walls, King Hezekiah's message was straightforward: "We trust in the LORD our God. The LORD will deliver us."

From outside the walls, the taunts of the messenger from Sennacherib, king of Assyria, were terrifying: "You're doomed to eat your own dung and drink your own urine." At the heart of the taunts was an effort to undermine the people's trust in their king and faith in their God.

> "Do not let Hezekiah deceive you, for he will not be able to deliver you." (36.14)

> "Do not let Hezekiah make you trust in the LORD by saying, 'The LORD will surely deliver us.'" (36.15)

> "Do not listen to Hezekiah. For thus says the king of Assyria: Make your peace with me and come out to me." (36.16)

Don't listen, don't follow, don't trust in the LORD. Spoiler alert: by the end of Isaiah 37, the LORD is exalted and Sennacherib's army is decimated. But thousands of years later, the taunts and pressures haven't let up, have they? Don't listen, don't follow, don't trust in the LORD.

It's interesting how a more familiar New Testament passage provides an ever-relevant answer to the taunts, "so that (our) faith might not rest in the wisdom of men but in the power of God."

> Yet among the mature we do impart wisdom, although it is not a wisdom of this age or of the rulers of this age, who are doomed to pass away. But we impart a secret and hidden wisdom of God, which God decreed before the ages for our glory. None of the rulers of this age understood this, for if they had, they would not have crucified the Lord of glory. But, as it is written,
>
> "What no eye has seen, nor ear heard,
>     nor the heart of man imagined,
> what God has prepared for those who love him"—
>
> these things God has revealed to us through the Spirit. (1 Cor 2.5–10)

And so we too find ourselves at the crossroads. The spirit of those taunts shouted centuries ago outside Jerusalem lives on: don't listen, don't follow, don't trust in God. How foolish to allow the Bible to define and regulate issues of sexuality, marriage, morality, ethics, righteousness, and self-control in the 21st century! It's past time to make your peace with the wisdom of this age.

But the Spirit who is from God continues to draw our attention and allegiance heavenward. To whom will we listen? What will we believe? In whom will our trust and confidence rest? Will we walk by sight or by faith?

Each of us makes that choice at the crossroads daily. Choose wisely.

# THURSDAY

*Bringing Children to Jesus Is Never a Wasted Effort*

Slow down and take the time to really read this scene from Jesus' life:

> They were bringing children to him that he might touch them, and the disciples rebuked them. But when Jesus saw it, he was indignant and said to them, "Let the children come to me; do not hinder them, for to such belongs the kingdom of God. Truly, I say to you, whoever does not receive the kingdom of God like a child shall not enter it." And he took them in his arms and blessed them, laying his hands on them. (Mark 10.13–16)

Think about that scene, **young mom** or **dad**. You got home last night after Bible class and you were exhausted. You barely had time to feed the family *before* class, getting to the church building was hectic, and getting everyone home and in bed was the icing on the cake of a chaotic day. Was it worth it? Hear Jesus say, "Let the children come to me."

Think about that scene, **Bible class teacher**. You worked all day and while other adults were vegetating in front of the TV, you were singing "Jesus Loves Me" to a bunch of toddlers for the thousandth time. Was it worth it? Envision Jesus taking children in his arms and blessing them.

Think about that scene, **shepherds** and **deacons** and **preachers** who are in the thick of planning how best to serve and lead your brothers and sisters. Maybe it's an incredibly busy time and it would be easy to push children's Bible classes to the back burner. Aren't there more important things? More pressing matters? Does excellence really matter when it comes to 7- and 8-year-olds? Hear Jesus say, "Don't hinder the children, for to such belongs the kingdom of God. Truly, I say to you, whoever does not receive the kingdom of God like a child shall not enter it."

Bringing children face-to-face with Jesus is never a wasted effort.

Take heart, young parent. Be encouraged, dedicated Bible class teacher. Press on, servant who is leading God's people through the next challenge. Shaping hearts for God is the most important work in the world.

# FRIDAY

## *The Preventative Power of Patience*

There's a whole lot of grumbling, complaining, disputing, and doubting in the Old Testament book of *Numbers*. The instance in Numbers 21 is interesting because it tells us *why* the people grumbled.

> From Mount Hor they set out by the way to the Red Sea, to go around the land of Edom. **And the people became impatient on the way.** And the people spoke against God and against Moses, "Why have you brought us up out of Egypt to die in the wilderness? For there is no food and no water, and we loathe this worthless food." (Num 21.4–5)

The people became impatient. Do *we* not grapple with the same tendency? Notice, when people become impatient:

- **They lose sight of the "Why?"** – "Why have you brought us up out of Egypt?" Answer: to bring you into the Promised Land. But due to impatience, the "Why?" wasn't clear.
- **Faith is replaced with despair** – "Why have you brought us up out of Egypt to die in the wilderness?" Don't miss the sad irony; this question is addressed to the Sender of the plagues, the Institutor of the Passover, the Parter of the Red Sea, the Provider of manna from heaven and water from wilderness rocks. Faith had eroded into despair.

- **They vent the ingratitude that has filled their hearts** – "For there is no food and no water, and we loathe this worthless food." Is it not a supremely dangerous thing to call what God has provided "worthless"?

Don't miss the fact that centuries later, Christians are warned by the Holy Spirit about the same pitfall?

> Be patient, therefore, brothers and sisters, until the coming of the Lord. See how the farmer waits for the precious fruit of the earth, being patient about it, until it receives the early and the late rains. You also, be patient. Establish your hearts, for the coming of the Lord is at hand. Do not grumble against one another, brothers, so that you may not be judged; behold, the Judge is standing at the door. (James 5.7–9)

**Be patient.** Teach your children to be patient. **Why?**

- Without patience, we lose sight of the "Why?" — the coming of the Lord is at hand.
- Without patience, faith is replaced with despair — establish your hearts.
- Without patience, ingratitude fills our hearts, and that's a very big deal because "the Judge is standing at the door."

Be patient, therefore, brothers and sisters, until the coming of the Lord. Let's work on that today.

# SATURDAY

## *"Be Strengthened"*

You then, my child, be strengthened by the grace that is in Christ Jesus. (2 Tim 2.1)

That's a thought worth turning over in your mind throughout the day. Strength is available. It's not strength *within* you or me. It's the strength of grace that is available in Christ Jesus. You can "be strengthened" by Someone beyond yourself today.

How? How's that work? Notice two tracks from 2 Timothy 2– things to avoid and things to pursue.

**First, things to AVOID:**

Charge them before God not to quarrel about words, which does no good, but only ruins the hearers. (2.14)

Avoid irreverent babble, for it will lead people into more and more ungodliness. (2.16)

Have nothing to do with foolish, ignorant controversies; you know that they breed quarrels. (2.23)

Do you want to be strengthened by the grace that is in Christ Jesus today? Don't quarrel. Steer clear of irreverent babble. Have nothing to do with foolish, ignorant controversies. Why? Because they ruin the hearers. They lead into the tunnel of ungodliness. They breed quarrels. They don't strengthen us or build others up because they flow in the opposite direction of grace.

**But there are also things to PURSUE:**

So flee youthful passions and pursue righteousness, faith, love, and peace, along with those who call on the Lord from a pure heart. (2.22)

Strength is available today. It's not strength *within* you or me. It's the strength of grace that is available in Jesus. You can "be strengthened" today, but you have to trust that Christ knows what he's talking about when he tells you to avoid the foolishness of this world and pursue what will build you up and encourage others.

God's firm foundation stands, bearing this seal: "The Lord knows those who are his," and, "Let everyone who names the name of the Lord depart from iniquity." (2.19)

Let's act like those who are his today.

# WEEK SEVEN

## SUNDAY

### *Are You Thirsty?*

"A Psalm of David, When He Was in the Wilderness of Judah." That bit of context is significant in Psalm 63. The Judean wilderness is harsh territory—scarce food, even scarcer water. But notice what David wrote in Psalm 63.5.

> My soul will be satisfied as with fat and rich food,
> and my mouth will praise you with joyful lips…

How could anyone say such a thing in the desert? It all depends upon the **source** of the satisfaction.

> O God, you are my God; earnestly I seek you;
> my soul thirsts for you;
> my flesh faints for you,
> as in a dry and weary land where there is no water.
> So I have looked upon you in the sanctuary,
> beholding your power and glory.
> Because your steadfast love is better than life,
> my lips will praise you. (Psa 63.1–3)

Many woke up this morning to a desolate wasteland of the soul. They feel isolated and hopeless. They're wondering what the point of it all is. They've trudged from one happiness-mirage to another and repeatedly ended up with handfuls of sand. They're bitter, calloused, and pessimistic.

If that's you today, you need to know that your Creator can make water flow in the dry stream beds of the most parched soul. He's done it over and over again. Real transformation and abundant satisfaction are freely available. Here's the question: **Are you thirsty?** Not just casually thirsty, looking for refreshment on your own terms, but **soul-thirsty**; thirsty to the point of being desperate—ready and eager to "cling" to God (Psa 63.8) as the greatest treasure, the most satisfying reality in the universe?

Whomever you are, wherever you've been, the gracious Giver of living water knows and cares. He's willing and able to refresh you. **Come thirsty.** Earnestly seek him, and you won't be disappointed. The water he gives becomes a spring of the soul, welling up to eternal life.

# MONDAY

## *The Subtle Danger That Comes With Being "At Ease"*

"In the thought of one who is at ease there is contempt for misfortune…" (Job 12.5)

"At ease" is a great place to be on a Monday. You worked hard last week and kept your nose to the grindstone. Maybe you kicked back, relaxed, and enjoyed the weekend. Then, to be "at ease" on a Monday? That's a great place to be.

"At ease" is a great place to be in life. Your career is going well, your marriage is great, the kids are healthy, there's money in the bank, and the future couldn't be more bright.

"At ease" is a great place to be as a nation. Sure, there are the daily headlines that worry us here and there, but year in and year out we lead such comfortable lives. We have incredible modern conveniences, we enjoy wonderful freedoms, and we're citizens of a country where opportunities abound.

"At ease" is a great place to be.

But take a moment to chew on what Job said a long, long time ago. "In the thought of one who is at ease there is contempt for misfortune." What is it about the "good life" that can so subtly intoxicate and delude us into believing we have the right to look down on the less fortunate? Why in the world would I ever look at my ease as license to despise those who are downtrodden and hurting? Why am I, in my present ease, worthy of more respect than the person in present need?

It makes me think of those two men from Jesus's parable in Luke 16.

> "There was a rich man who was clothed in purple and fine linen and who feasted sumptuously every day. And at his gate was laid a poor man named Lazarus, covered with sores, who desired to be fed with what fell from the rich man's table. Moreover, even the dogs came and licked his sores..." (Luke 16.19–21)

Why should that rich man pay any attention to some poor fellow that had been laid at his gate? He was "at ease." Fancy clothes. Gated property. Sumptuous feasts, day after day after day. In the thoughts of the one who was at ease there was a lack of concern for misfortune...

...but then the rich man died.

And in Hades he was reminded, "you in your lifetime received your good things, and Lazarus in like manner bad things; but now he is comforted here, and you are in anguish" (Luke 16.25).

"At ease" in life, but "in anguish" for eternity? That's a bad trade.

One of the great lessons in the Old Testament book of *Job* is that we ought to be so very careful "explaining" things far above our pay grade. Why are some "at ease" while others are "in anguish"? Why do some live for decades in the lap of luxury while others continually struggle to provide the most basic necessities? Why are some born in prosperous countries and others born into nightmarish environments? We don't know.

But here's one thing we *should* know and remember: in the thoughts of those at ease, there ought not be any contempt for misfortune. We're channels, not reservoirs. We've been blessed to bless. Comforted to comfort. Saved to serve. We don't look down on, we lift up in the name of the One who was despised and rejected that we might be forgiven, reconciled, and transformed. We reflect a holy light. We share in the name of the Savior who has gone to prepare a place for us. We bear each other's burdens in the name of the King who is coming again.

"At ease" is a great place to be on a Monday. But let's not be so "at ease" that contempt begins to choke our hearts. May gratitude, compassion, and generosity fill our thoughts and fuel our service today.

# TUESDAY

*Building Good Reputations: Block by Block,*
*Day by Day*

In Acts 6, a complaint arose among some of the Greek-speaking Jews because their widows were being neglected. Notice the apostles' response:

> "It is not right that we should give up preaching the word of God to serve tables. Therefore, brothers, pick out from among you seven men **of good repute**, full of the Spirit and of wisdom, whom we will appoint to this duty." (Acts 6.1–3)

**"Of good repute."** These men needed to have good reputations. They were expected to have *already* demonstrated character, humility, honesty, and maturity. If this opportunity were the first time that Stephen, Philip, or any of the others gave serious thought to their reputations, it would already be too late. The past of these men was what had led them to be qualified to serve in the present.

We obviously don't live in the era of Acts 6, but each one of us—male and female, young and old—is building a reputation, block by block, day by day.

Your reputation is being shaped by how you conduct yourself on social media: what you share, how you comment, what you like.

My reputation is being molded by my treatment of the people around me, my priorities, punctuality, and whether I keep my promises.

Decision-by-decision, reaction-by-reaction, mood-by-mood, post-by-post, encounter-by-encounter, each one of us is building a reputation. That makes the wisdom of Proverbs 22.1 worth chewing on today:

> A good name is to be chosen rather than great riches,
>     and favor is better than silver or gold.

You can't purchase "good repute" on Amazon. I can't download a "good name" in any App store. But who knows what future opportunities could be extended to us or doors be closed on us based on the choices we make this week?

Does that sobering reality mean my past will forever define and mar my future? Not in Christ. Paul could write about "formerly" being a persecutor (1 Tim 1.13). "Such were some of you" was an accurate description of men and women in Corinth who had been washed, sanctified, justified in the name of the Lord Jesus Christ and by the Spirit of our God (1 Cor 6.9–11).

You've heard that old Chinese proverb? "The best time to plant a tree was 20 years ago. The second best time is now." Just so, the best time to start looking carefully how you walk, not as unwise but as wise, was 20 years ago. The second best time is now.

Life is connected. Steps form paths and paths produce reputations. As much as depends on us, let's be men and women "of good repute, full of the Spirit and of wisdom" today.

# WEDNESDAY

## *In What Direction is Your Camp Facing?*

Numbers 2 is full of ... numbers. Throughout the chapter, the LORD is communicating to Moses and Aaron how the people of Israel—probably about two million people in all—were to arrange camp as they passed through the wilderness on their way to the Promised Land. It's easy to get lost as we read about which tribe is to camp in which direction, but notice Numbers 2.2:

> "The people of Israel shall camp each by his own standard, with the banners of their fathers' houses. They shall camp facing the tent of meeting on every side."

Picture two million people broken into twelve tribes with three tribes camped in each direction—east, south, west, and north. And in the center of it all, the Tabernacle—the tent of meeting—where the LORD God Almighty had promised to dwell among his people. Imagine the clusters of small camps, as far as the eye can see, covering the sands of the wilderness. But each and every camp is intentionally arranged to face the tent of meeting. God is the heart, the hub, the focal point of his people.

We obviously live in very different circumstances. You didn't wake up this morning in the wilderness of Sinai. You didn't go outside looking for manna in your front yard. But your "camp" ... in what direction is it facing? What's the focal point of your home? What influence shapes the beginning of each day? Whose presence dictates the direction of your week?

Some of us, first thing in the morning, check every social media feed several times over before prayer even crosses our minds. Some of us turn on *The Today Show* or *SportsCenter* long before we feed ourselves with the living word of God. Some of us spend hours Netflix-binging and somehow convince ourselves that we don't have time, day by day, to sustain and fortify our souls. Some of us distract ourselves with the noise of this world through our last waking moments ... and then we do it all over again the next day.

How long would these millions of Israelites lived in the wilderness without manna from heaven? And honestly, how long can our souls thrive in the spiritual wasteland that is this world if we consistently neglect the life-giving words that come from the mouth of God (Matt 4.4)? Living water is freely available (John 4.10), but how often have I (intentionally or unintentionally) faced the challenges of the day, day after day, without it?

God was the unmistakable focal point of Israel's physical camp. It was a simple, daily reminder that he was to be the life-giving heartbeat of everything.

In what direction is *your* camp facing?

# THURSDAY

## *Called. Loved. Kept.*

**Called. Loved. Kept.** This is how we ought to think of ourselves as disciples of Jesus today. Above and beyond the color of our skin, the level of our education, the size of our bank account, or what we do for a living, "I am called. I am loved. I am kept."

> Jude, a servant of Jesus Christ and brother of James, To those who are **called, beloved** in God the Father and **kept** for Jesus Christ: May mercy, peace, and love be multiplied to you. (Jude 1–2)

Notice how those first two verses of Jude's little letter in the New Testament correspond with the last two verses of his letter:

> Now to him who is able to keep you from stumbling and to present you blameless before the presence of his glory with great joy, to the only God, our Savior, through Jesus Christ our Lord, be glory, majesty, dominion, and authority, before all time and now and forever. Amen. (Jude 24–25)

Put it all together and you've got a Spirit-shaped lens to help you see as God sees today.

**I am called**, called to glorify my Creator by recognizing, submitting to, and magnifying his "glory, majesty, dominion, and authority." He is "the only God," before all time, now, and forever. I am called—as his creation—to honor him.

**I am loved**, loved "in God the Father" who loved me first and gave his Son for me so that I, an unworthy sinner, might be presented "blameless before the presence of his glory with great joy." What more could he do to show how much he cares?

**I am kept,** kept for Jesus Christ my Lord, the good Shepherd who is able to "keep me from stumbling" if I will follow his lead, listen to his warnings, and trust his promises. If he is for me, who can be against me?

**Called. Loved. Kept.** Above and beyond all the distractions, discouragements, and vanities of the day, this is who my Father says I am. This is how he wants me to see myself. "I am called. I am loved. I am kept." Today is my opportunity to show that I believe him and encourage others to do the same.

# FRIDAY

### *From Lamentation to "But" to "Therefore"*

For some, it's been a lamentable week. For many, it's been a lamentable month. For you, maybe it's even been a lamentable year. Have you ever read the Old Testament book of *Lamentations*? What help for perspective could possibly come from a book of the Bible with a title like that?

Lamentations 5, uses words like *disgrace*, *weariness*, and *mourning*. "The joy of our hearts has ceased" (5.15) and "for these things our eyes have grown dim" (5.17). You get the idea.

**"But..."**

Here's something worth thinking about, especially if you're in a challenging season.

> But you, O LORD, reign forever;
> your throne endures to all generations. (5.19)

Even in a book full of laments, a light shines in the darkness. The writer is honest in his description of affliction, wanderings, wormwood, and gall. "My soul continually remembers it and is bowed down within me" (3.19–20). Maybe that sort of honesty resonates with you, right where you are.

**"But..."** There it is again.

> But this I call to mind,
> and therefore I have hope:

The steadfast love of the LORD never ceases;
   his mercies never come to an end;
they are new every morning;
   great is your faithfulness.
"The LORD is my portion," says my soul,
   "therefore I will hope in him." (3.21–24)

Live long enough, and you'll have lamentable days, weeks, months, even years. What says your soul in the toughest of times? Does it have an anchor? Is hope alive?

Every book of the Bible is worth reading and meditating upon, even a book with a title like *Lamentations*, because it reminds us that in the most difficult of times, our God is not absent. He is not socially distanced from his people. He is not locked down, restricted, or furloughed. His work has not stopped; in fact, it hasn't even been slowed. His mercies are never exhausted. They are new and fresh this very morning. His steadfast love never ceases. The weight of his faithfulness is greater than the weight of our griefs. His throne endures. He reigns today.

That's how lamentation leads to **"but"** leads to **"therefore."**

"The LORD is my portion," says my soul,
   "therefore I will hope in him."

Of all the books in all of the Bible, who would have guessed that *Lamentations* would remind us today that hope is alive, even in the darkest valleys?

# SATURDAY

## *The Light of the World Gave Darkness an Hour*

Luke 22 details a dark night of shortsighted disputes, heartbreaking predictions, multiple denials, and outright betrayal.

"As was his custom," Jesus had gone outside Jerusalem's walls to the Mount of Olives. Being in agony, he had withdrawn about a stone's throw from his disciples and prayed so earnestly that his sweat became like great drops of blood. When he rose from prayer, he found his disciples sleeping. "Why are you sleeping? Rise and pray that you may not enter into temptation."

> While he was still speaking, there came a crowd, and the man called Judas, one of the twelve, was leading them. He drew near to Jesus to kiss him, but Jesus said to him, "Judas, would you betray the Son of Man with a kiss?" And when those who were around him saw what would follow, they said, "Lord, shall we strike with the sword?" And one of them struck the servant of the high priest and cut off his right ear. But Jesus said, "No more of this!" And he touched his ear and healed him. Then Jesus said to the chief priests and officers of the temple and elders, who had come out against him, "Have you come out as against a robber, with swords and clubs? When I was with you day after day in the temple, you did not lay hands on me. **But this is your hour, and the power of darkness.**" (Luke 22.47–53)

**"This is your hour."** The Light of the world gave darkness an "hour" to unleash its Satanic worst in order that he (and we) might triumph over darkness and death for eternity.

Jesus yielded to an **"hour"** of darkness so that I could be adopted as a child of light.

Jesus yielded to an **"hour"** of betrayal so that your treason could be pardoned.

Jesus yielded to an **"hour"** of captivity so that I could be set free.

Jesus yielded to an **"hour"** of mocking so that you could hear, "Welcome home, good and faithful servant."

Jesus yielded to an **"hour"** of beatings so that I could be healed.

Jesus yielded to an **"hour"** of shame so that you might not have to be ashamed.

Jesus yielded to an **"hour"** on the cross so that my body of sin might be brought to nothing.

Jesus yielded to an **"hour"** in the grave so that you might be raised to walk in newness of life.

Darkness had an **"hour,"** and because Jesus yielded to that "hour," we have living hope.

Whatever you're enduring today, remember: the power of darkness may rage for an "hour," but the day is coming when it will be banished forever by inexpressible light. Death has its "hour," but it will ultimately be swallowed up by life eternal. Our adversaries at their absolute worst are no match for the Lord whose grave is still empty.

> "He will wipe away every tear from their eyes, and death shall be no more, neither shall there be mourning, nor crying, nor pain anymore, for the former things have passed away." (Rev 21.4)

Ten thousand years from now, against the brilliant backdrop of eternal life and light and love, how brief the darkest "hour" will seem to have been…

# WEEK EIGHT

## SUNDAY

### *A Quiet, Reverent Look in the Rearview Mirror*

I love the Psalms of the Bible for a variety of reasons, one being the fact that just about every human emotion is represented, wrestled with, and channeled back into the ups and downs of everyday life with God-shaped perspective.

Fear. Anger. Frustration. Despair. Guilt. You don't have to turn many pages in the Psalms before you encounter each one of those feelings, and in the encounter, you're reminded that you are not alone. Many before you have known what it is to grapple with each one of those emotions.

But what will I *do* with those very real feelings in the present? Where will I turn for perspective, guidance, refuge, and hope when fear, anger, frustration, despair, and guilt are knocking on the front door of my heart?

Answers and approaches vary.

Some of us look to the **present**—the fleeting, fickle, ever-shifting present—as a means of coping with what we're feeling. We'll distract ourselves with social media. We'll detach ourselves with mindless smartphone games. We'll incessantly occupy ourselves with the latest "news" or seek to pacify ourselves with another instant download. In short, many of us fill our present with noise in an attempt to divert attention away from what's going on in our hearts.

Some of us look to the **future**—the always-promising, rarely-delivering future—in an attempt to deal with what we're feeling. If we can just get to the next road trip, or the next promotion, or the bigger house... If we can finally reach the dream getaway, the shinier car, the perfect relationship, the next rung in the ladder...

...and all-the-while, the noise I'm surrounding myself with doesn't build my sense of peace or clarify my perspective. The ever-elusive future isn't settling my heart or galvanizing my hope, and heaviness in the present remains.

Am I missing something? If what I need to cope, endure, and thrive isn't in the distractions of a noisy **present** or the dreams of a self-centered **future**, where else can I turn? Is it possible for the answer to be preserved in the **past**?

In Psalm 61, David was wrestling with a very heavy present. It felt like life had taken him to "the end of the earth." His heart was "faint" (61.2). He had a keen sense of present need. He *needed* to be led "to the rock" that was higher than himself. He was presently *in need* of "refuge under the shelter" of another's wings (61.4).

So how did he cope? In Psalm 61, David didn't attempt to drown those emotions with distractions or dilute those feelings with bigger and better dreams of an unrealistic future. He processed those very real feelings in the light of what God had done in the past.

"My heart is faint" (61.2)—present tense—but "you **have been** my refuge, a strong tower against the enemy" (61.3).

"Let me take refuge" (61.4)—present tense—"for you, O God, **have heard** my vows; you **have given** me the heritage of those who fear your name" (61.5).

And by the end of the psalm, David has found solid ground on which to stand, in the present. His immediate circumstances might be beyond his control, his future may yet be unclear, but blessed assurance is abundantly available because he has reminded himself of God's faithfulness in the past. "So," despite the swirl of present emotions and future obstacles, "I will ever sing praises to your name, as I perform my vows day after day" (61.8).

If you're like me, you find it very easy to begin and fill and end your day with the vain noise of the present and fruitless worries about the future. What if—let's say tomorrow morning—we did a little bit of Bible reading, taking a quiet, reverent look to the past before we filled our minds with the noise of the present and blind predictions about the future? What if we spent a few moments praising God for what he **has** done before we tackled our to-do lists? What if we thanked him anew for the prayers he **has** answered and used those as fuel for taking future steps with him in confidence? What if we stopped presuming on the riches of his kindness and forbearance and patience and we just did the next right thing, for the sake of his name, day after day?

I'm guessing, if we did that, we'd find it easier—more natural even—to "ever sing praises to his name," regardless of how chaotic the present may seem in the moment. And in the future? Perhaps we'd see more clearly the One who has been closer to us, all along, than we ever imagined.

# MONDAY

## *To What (or Whom) Are Hurtful People Driving You?*

1 Samuel 1 documents a heart-breaking situation. A man named Elkanah had two wives—Hannah and Peninnah. Peninnah had children, Hannah did not. Every year at the time of sacrifice to the LORD of hosts, Elkanah would give portions to Peninnah and to all her sons and daughters, but to Hannah he would give a double portion, "because he loved her."

> And her rival used to provoke [Hannah] grievously to irritate her, because the LORD had closed her womb. So it went on year by year. As often as she went up to the house of the LORD, [Peninnah] used to provoke [Hannah]. Therefore Hannah wept and would not eat. (1 Sam 1.6–7)

Some people are just mean. Plain and simple. They boast. They're arrogant and rude. They enjoy rivalry. They will go out of their way to irritate. They're skilled at crushing the spirits of others. They walk in the footsteps of Peninnah.

If you find yourself in the place of Hannah today, here's a question worth thinking about: **"To what (or whom) is that hurtful person driving me?"** Some of us in Hannah's position are driven to bitterness and isolation. Some of us attempt to mask the hurt with artificial, sometimes foolish "fixes." Others of us are driven to deep-seated wrath and revenge.

Take a moment to admire and learn from Hannah today. Her rival used to provoke her grievously with one aim: to irritate. It went on, year after year after year.

And it drove Hannah towards God.

> She was deeply distressed and prayed to the LORD and wept bitterly. (1 Sam 1.10)

To what (or whom) are hurtful people driving you?

# TUESDAY

## *Beloved, Prepare for War*

Beloved, I urge you as sojourners and exiles to abstain from the passions of the flesh, which wage war against your soul. (1 Pet 2.11)

You are at war today—*you*, as an individual, whether you recognize it or not. In fact, you were born into a world at war—an ancient, ongoing war. Human hearts are the battleground and yours is no exception. War has been declared "against your soul."

That's rough news for a Tuesday morning. Want some good news? Look at the first word in 1 Peter 2.11. "Beloved." You are loved. You aren't in this war alone. The Savior and King who is leading his disciples to victory is "clothed in a robe dipped in blood" (Rev 19.13)—his own blood, shed for those he loved enough to ransom. He is the ultimate Victor. Read his revelation. We've already been told how this war is going to end.

What matters in the meantime is that we pledge our allegiance to him, follow his lead, live with the mindset of "sojourners and exiles" and "abstain from the passions of the flesh" which are waging war against our souls.

**And there's the mindset we need as a new week is still unfolding.** Our hearts are the battleground. War is being waged against our souls. Temptations will come in blatant and subtle ways this week, luring the passions of our flesh, enticing us to spurn our Savior and abandon our rightful King.

You are at war. Sexual immorality is waging war against your love and joy. Impurity and sensuality are waging war against your self-control. Idolatry is waging war against your faithfulness. Enmity, strife, jealousy, anger, rivalry, dissension, division, and envy are waging war against your gentleness, goodness, kindness, patience, and peace.

We've lost on those fronts before, but past defeats don't have to define our present or destroy our future. Look to your conquering King, clothed in a bloody robe.

> He himself bore our sins in his body on the tree, that we might die to sin and live to righteousness. By his wounds you have been healed. For you were straying like sheep, but have now returned to the Shepherd and Overseer of your souls. (1 Pet 2.24–25)

Beloved, listen to his urgings today. Walk like a sojourner and exile this week. This world is not your home, don't act like it is. Abstain from the passions of the flesh which can cost you your soul. Don't be heaven-bound in theory. Live as a heaven-bound conqueror, set free by the blood of Jesus, standing strong in the strength that he supplies.

# WEDNESDAY

## *"There I Will Meet With You"*

The third book of the Bible begins on an awesome note.

> The LORD called Moses and spoke to him from the tent of meeting… (Leviticus 1.1)

The tabernacle that Moses and the people had constructed according to the God-given pattern in *Exodus* was consistently referred to as "the tent of meeting." The LORD had promised:

> "There I will meet with you, and from above the mercy seat, from between the two cherubim that are on the ark of the testimony, I will speak with you about all that I will give you in commandment for the people of Israel." (Exo 25.22)

And so, at the opening of *Leviticus*, the LORD fulfilled his promise, calling Moses and speaking to him from "the tent of meeting."

Take a moment to marvel at the fact that the same God continues to call and speak, not from within an ornate tent, but through his "living and active" word (Heb 4.12). Meditate on the fact that you and I can see more clearly, discern more fully, and connect more dots concerning the LORD's accomplishments than Moses could have possibly imagined (1 Pet 1.10–12).

When you open your Bible today, think of it as a "book of meeting." You are opening your heart and mind to the voice of God.

When you pray today, think of it as a "moment of meeting." In the name of Jesus, the eternal high priest, you've been invited to draw near to the throne of grace with confidence.

When you observe the Lord's Supper this Sunday, think of it as the "body and blood of meeting." You are communing with the Lord and his people, proclaiming his death until he comes.

The Lord called Moses and spoke to him from "the tent of meeting" in Leviticus 1. "There I will meet with you." We have no earthly tabernacle, but God's incredible promise continues to live on in the hearts of those with eyes to see and ears to hear.

# THURSDAY

### *"Tell Them How Much the Lord Has Done for You"*

"What should I say? How should I start?" Those are common questions for disciples of Jesus.

"I'm a new Christian and I want to positively influence my friends and family, but I don't know what to say."

"It's been a long time since I tried to share the gospel with anyone and I'm not sure where to begin."

"I'm afraid if I bring Jesus up, someone will ask me a question I can't answer."

If you've ever felt those hesitancies before, Mark 5 is worth thinking about today. Mark 5.1–20 tells us of Jesus healing a severely demon-possessed man. Afterwards, "as Jesus was getting into the boat, the man who had been possessed with demons begged him that he might be with him. And he did not permit him but said to him, 'Go home to your friends and tell them how much the Lord has done for you, and how he has had mercy on you'" (Mark 5.18–19).

**"Tell them how much the Lord has done for you…"** Can you do that?

- "I was struggling to understand what life was all about, but Jesus…"
- "That addiction was slowly destroying my marriage, but Jesus…"

- "For a long time I was really struggling with selfishness, but Jesus…"
- "I never thought I'd be able to leave my past behind, but Jesus…"
- "I really worried about raising kids in this world, but Jesus…"

You might not be able to answer every question. You might have only taken a few steps as a disciple. You might not have tried to start a conversation about the Bible in a long time. Okay, but the next time that door of opportunity opens right before your eyes, remember Mark 5. "Tell them how much the Lord has done for you." That's a great place to start.

# FRIDAY

## *Private Information: The Currency of Gossips, Whisperers, Slanderers, and Busybodies*

How do you handle private information? Here's one pathway: private information is **currency**, something I can use for my own personal gain. I introduce the possibility of exchanging this currency with:

- "Did you hear?"
- "Did you see?"
- "Did you know?"

I treat private information as currency in order to:

- Gain access to a certain crowd of people
- Buy temporary attention
- Create conversational wiggle-room to shift uncomfortable attention away from myself
- Purchase a shot of depraved adrenaline for my twisted, self-serving heart (Matt 15.19)

Private information is treated as currency by gossips (Rom 1.29), whisperers (Prov 18.8), slanderers (Eph 4.31), and busybodies (1 Tim 5.13).

How do *you* handle private information? Here's a distinctly different pathway.

Private information is frequently **a call** for prayer (James 5.16).

Private information is often **a confession,** the fruit of a heart that has turned in genuine repentance and thereby opened up the possibility for healing (Matt 18.15).

Private information periodically reveals **a case** (Prov 16.28) to be handled with utmost **care** (Heb 12.12–13) and loving **concern** (2 Thes 3.15). It very well may involve **confrontation** (2 Sam 12.7). The goal of the confrontation is **conviction** (2 Sam 12.13) in order that the wayward man or woman will make a **confession** as an indispensable first step toward healing (James 5.19–20).

How do you handle private information?

Whereas private information is treated as currency by gossips, whisperers, slanderers, and busybodies, our heavenly Father calls us to recognize that private information so very often presents an opportunity for prayer, confession, care, concern, and, if need be, confrontation.

Framed from a slightly different angle, treating the private information of another as currency is all about *me.* Wisely handling the private information of another as a call for fervent prayer, the delicate fruit of a contrite heart, or an occasion for loving care and selfless concern is all about treating *others* as I would like to be treated (Matt 7.12).

> Whoever covers an offense **seeks** love,
>     but he who repeats a matter separates close friends. (Prov 17.9)

How do *you* handle private information? It's ultimately a question of what you are **seeking.** Is private information currency to be used *by* you or an opportunity *for* you to serve someone else?

# SATURDAY

## *On Seeing Them...*

And so we came to Rome. And the brothers there, when they heard about us, came as far as the Forum of Appius and Three Taverns to meet us. On seeing them, Paul thanked God and took courage. (Acts 28.14–15)

I'm thankful for websites and livestreams and video conferencing. I'm sure Paul was thankful for parchment and ink and faithful messengers to carry his letters to the churches. His epistle to the church in Rome had arrived three years before he did in the flesh. Now, finally—after months and more than a thousand miles on the Mediterranean—Paul saw these brothers and sisters with his own eyes.

"I long to see you," he had written in Romans 1.11–12, "that I may impart to you some spiritual gift to strengthen you—that is, that we may be mutually encouraged by each other's faith, both yours and mine." John knew the feeling. "Though I have much to write to you, I would rather not use paper and ink. Instead I hope to come to you and talk face to face, so that our joy may be complete" (2 John 12).

I'm thankful for those letters. I'm thankful for the ancient innovations that made them possible. And I'm thankful for the wonders of modern technology. Can you imagine what John would say about email or how the heart of Paul would explode at the possibility of connecting with brethren via live video?

And yet, even 2,000 years later, it's not the same as seeing each other with our own eyes. Face to face. I have hundreds of hymn tracks on my phone, but it's not the same as the mutual encouragement that comes from singing "in the midst of the congregation." High definition video can't compete with the joy of physical presence… hearing Bible pages turn and little babies cry… seeing tears of conviction roll down cheeks and couples who've been married more than 50 years still holding hands in worship.

Paul, John, and others used paper and ink, and I'm glad they did. We use lenses and computers, and I'm thankful for them. But an indispensable aspect of joy is made "complete" only when God's children are face to face.

So much of the disciple's walk is "by faith, not by sight." Though we have not seen Jesus, we love him. "Though you do not now see him, you believe in him and rejoice with joy that is inexpressible and filled with glory, obtaining the outcome of your faith, the salvation of your souls" (1 Pet 1.8–9). One day, we "will see his face" (Rev 22.4).

In the meantime, like Paul as he traveled the last few miles to Rome, we thank God for fellowship and foretastes of glory. And we take courage.

# WEEK NINE

## SUNDAY

### *"Open the Gates!"*

In the ancient world, when kings approached, gates were opened. David, the author of Psalm 24, understood that. He himself was a king. But in Psalm 24, David isn't the hero. He poetically describes the approach of a greater King. The *greatest* King.

> Lift up your heads, O gates!
>> And be lifted up, O ancient doors,
>> that the King of glory may come in.
> Who is this King of glory?
>> The LORD of hosts,
>> he is the King of glory! (Psa 24.9–10)

When the King of glory approaches, gates should certainly open.

Christians around the world are gathering on this first day of the week with a glorious anthem in their hearts. "O worship the King, all-glorious above, and gratefully sing His wonderful love; our Shield and Defender, the Ancient of Days, pavilioned in splendor and girded with praise" (Robert Grant, 1833).

This King of glory deserves access to everything. "The earth is the LORD's and everything that fills it, the world and those who dwell therein" (Psa 24.1). What does he desire to see in me? "Clean hands and a pure heart" (Psa 24.4). I haven't always given this King what he deserves. And yet, this first day of the week is full of hope.

"According to his great mercy," the King has graciously extended the opportunity for all to be "born again to a living hope through the resurrection of Jesus Christ from the dead" (1 Pet 1.3).

**Born again.** Minds which were once closed in self-centeredness can be opened to this King and set on things above, where Christ is (Col 3.1–2). Hearts which were once corrupt can be cleansed and used as instruments of praise and thanksgiving to his majesty (Eph 5.19–20). Bodies in which sin once reigned (Rom 6.12) can be presented as living sacrifices, holy and acceptable to the King (Rom 12.1). This is "living hope," freely available to all through the resurrection of Jesus from the dead.

So let's open the gates of praise and thanksgiving today. Open the gates of your love and allegiance "that the King of glory may come in" and reign on the throne of your heart.

# MONDAY

## *When the Messenger is Mocked*

Sometimes, people just don't want to listen to truth.

> When Jeremiah finished speaking to all the people all these words
> of the LORD their God, with which the LORD their God had sent
> him to them… (Jer 43.1)

Slow down for a moment and think about that language. The
LORD, the greatest reality in the universe, had a message for people
who only existed because he willed them to exist. He sent Jeremiah
with the message, and Jeremiah faithfully delivered the message.

> When Jeremiah finished speaking to all the people all these words
> of the LORD their God, with which the LORD their God had sent
> him to them, Azariah the son of Hoshaiah and Johanan the son of
> Kareah and all the insolent men said to Jeremiah, "You are telling
> a lie." (Jer 43.1–2)

Sometimes, people just don't want to listen to truth. Sometimes, they'll be ugly to the messenger. Sometimes, it'll go even
further. Sometimes, it'll cost the messenger everything…

…but will it really? Is the loss of a job, or a friendship, or a
family connection "everything"? Is the loss of social standing in
the eyes of people uninterested in truth "everything"? Is even the
loss of one's life "everything"?

Beloved, do not be surprised at the fiery trial when it comes upon you to test you, as though something strange were happening to you. But rejoice insofar as you share Christ's sufferings, that you may also rejoice and be glad when his glory is revealed. If you are insulted for the name of Christ, you are blessed, because the Spirit of glory and of God rests upon you. But let none of you suffer as a murderer or a thief or an evildoer or as a meddler. Yet if anyone suffers as a Christian, let him not be ashamed, but let him glorify God in that name. For it is time for judgment to begin at the household of God; and if it begins with us, what will be the outcome for those who do not obey the gospel of God? And

"If the righteous is scarcely saved,
    what will become of the ungodly and the sinner?"

Therefore let those who suffer according to God's will entrust their souls to a faithful Creator while doing good. (1 Pet 4.12–19)

Sometimes, people just don't want to listen to truth. That can be hard, in the moment, on the messenger. But we ought not be surprised. The warnings and examples are thousands of years old.

So let's be humble. Let's be diligent in examining the Scriptures daily, entrusting our souls to our faithful Creator. Let's be quick to hear, slow to speak, and slow to anger. Let's be doers of the word, not hearers or even sharers only.

And then? Let's be unashamed to speak and stand upon God-defined truth, whether people are willing to submit to it or not.

# TUESDAY

### *The One Who Has Been There Told Us So*

**"There is joy in heaven when…"**

Think about that amazing statement. Heaven is not an empty void, nor is it the make-believe stuff of fairytales. "Heaven is my throne," the LORD said in Isaiah 66.1.

And there is **joy** in heaven. Why? When? Over what? The answer might surprise you. Listen to Jesus in Luke 15:

> "I tell you, there will be more joy in heaven over one sinner who repents than over ninety-nine righteous persons who need no repentance." (15.7)

> "I tell you, there is joy before the angels of God over one sinner who repents." (15.10)

> "'…let us celebrate. For this my son was dead, and is alive again; he was lost, and is found.' And they began to celebrate." (15.23–24)

How could we possibly know what emotion is experienced in heaven when sinners on earth turn away from their sin? The *only* way we could know is if someone who had been in heaven told us.

In Luke 15, as Pharisees and scribes are grumbling about Jesus "receiving" tax collectors and sinners, the Son of God responds with three parables: a lost sheep, a lost coin, and a lost son. All three parables have a "lost" element on the front end; all three describe "joy" on the back end.

On earth, we sometimes struggle with how God will react if we're honest about our shortcomings and sins. Is he ashamed of me? Will he refuse my feeble efforts to turn things around? Have I forever blown it? Will he laugh in my face? Is it already too late to come home?

How could we possibly know how heaven feels and respods when sinners on earth repent? The *only* way is if someone who had been in heaven told us... **which is exactly what Jesus did in Luke 15.** The answer, in one word, is *joy*.

Do you know your heart is not right with your Creator? Do you know your transgressions have created a separation between you and the Giver of life? Don't let the fear of how God will react if you're honest about your shortcomings and sins keep you from doing what you need to do today. When we come to ourselves and take steps toward home, there is **joy** in heaven.

The One who has been there told us so.

# WEDNESDAY

## *How Do You Summarize an Incredible 120-Year-Life?*

120 years. If you lived to be 120-years-old, how would you want people to summarize your life? What few words, strung together, would mean the most?

The conclusion of the Bible's fifth book tells us about the death of Moses. He was 120 years old when he died (Deut 34.7). Just think of the phrases that could have been used to describe the incredible life of Moses. Prince of Egypt. Announcer of plagues. Nemesis of Pharaoh. Leader of millions. Dedicated judge. Covenant-mediator. Law-deliverer. Tabernacle-erector.

Each one of those phrases is amazing. Each one is a noteworthy thread in a tapestry 120 years in the making. But are these the best? The most outstanding? What few words, strung together, would mean the most?

I've never met Moses. I've watched over his shoulder in *Exodus*, listened to him in *Leviticus*, wandered with him in *Numbers*, and heard his last, heartfelt words in *Deuteronomy*. I feel like I know him, and I don't think he would be disappointed by the two simple phrases used to summarize his remarkable life—one in Deuteronomy 33 and one in Deuteronomy 34.

"Moses, the man of God…" (33.1)
"Moses, the servant of the Lord…" (34.5)

If you lived to be 120-years-old, how would you want people to summarize your life? What few words would mean the most? Real estate mogul? CEO of a Fortune 500 company? Millionaire? Billionaire? President of the United States? World-class athlete? Hollywood celebrity? Social media icon? Those are some remarkable phrases—the stuff of dreams for most. But are they the best? The most outstanding? Are there any words that would mean even more?

In light of eternity, there's no doubt about it. Man of God. Woman of God. Servant of the LORD. Ten thousand years from now, what phrases will mean more than those?

# THURSDAY

## *How to Speak With Confidence Today*

Keep your life free from love of money, and be content with what you have, for he has said, "I will never leave you nor forsake you." So we can confidently say,

> "The Lord is my helper;
>  I will not fear;
>  what can man do to me?" (Heb 13.5–6)

**He has said … so we can confidently say.** Do you see that? What a powerful reason to build the habit of reading God's word! When I open my Bible to *Genesis*, the psalms, or the gospels, I'm reading what "he has said." But my reading is to be so much more than a purely intellectual exercise. Reading by faith what *he* has said unlocks and opens the door to *me* saying, practicing, and enduring. *Confidently.* The source of my confidence is the Lord and what he has said. It's what Jesus described as building your life on the rock.

"I will never leave you nor forsake you" (Psa 118.6). So **we** can confidently say, "The Lord is my helper."

"Was it not necessary that the Christ should suffer these things and enter into his glory?" (Luke 24.26). So **we** can confidently proclaim, "The Lord has risen indeed."

"Repent and be baptized every one of you in the name of Jesus Christ for the forgiveness of your sins" (Acts 2.38). So **we** can confidently exhort, "Save yourselves from this crooked generation."

"Blessed is the man who remains steadfast under trial, for when he has stood the test he will receive the crown of life, which God has promised to those who love him" (James 1.12). So **we** can confidently sing, "May this journey bring a blessing, may I rise on wings of faith. At the end of my heart's testing, with your likeness let me wake."

"Surely I am coming soon" (Rev 22.20). So **we** can confidently pray, "Amen. Come, Lord Jesus!"

Do you want more confidence? Not the empty, self-made mask so many will walk around with today, but real, well-placed confidence in the right person for the right reasons? Open God's written revelation to mankind. Open your heart to what he has said. When he promises, you can be confident. "God is my helper. I'm not going to fear. If he is for me, who can be against me?"

# FRIDAY

## *Wrenches Don't Sing Their Own Praises*

My lawn and I have an appointment this evening. Time to mow. You know what's not going to happen? As I push the mower back into the garage, it's not going to boast about what it did for the last two hours.

I can be carried at 30,000 feet and more than 500 miles per hour, but I'm not going to hear the airplane magnify itself as I step off to retrieve my luggage.

Parking lots aren't full of chatter between Chevys and Fords, Hondas and Toyotas about what a fabulous job they did on this morning's commute.

They're all just tools. Some tools cost more than others, some are shiny and some are worn, but they're just tools. The lawn mower is pushed, the airplane is piloted, the automobile is driven, and we expect them to do what they were created to do. Once they've done so, tools don't boast.

In Isaiah 10, the awesome Assyrian empire is described as a rod in the LORD's hand. "Against a godless nation I send him, and against the people of my wrath I command him, to take spoil and seize plunder, and to tread them down like the mire of the streets" (10.5–6).

But the "rod" quickly forgets his place. In the arrogance of his heart, with a boastful look in his eyes, the king of Assyria says, "By the strength of my hand I have done it, and by my wisdom, for I have understanding; I remove the boundaries of peoples, and plunder their treasures; like a bull I bring down those who sit on thrones" (10.13).

And to God, that sounds about as foolish as my mower leading my shovel and rake in a chorus of self-exalting praise.

"Shall the axe boast over him who hews with it, or the saw magnify itself against him who wields it? As if a rod should wield him who lifts it, or as if a staff should lift him who is not wood" (10.15). When God had accomplished his purposes with the shortsighted "rod" of Assyria, his anger would be "directed to their destruction" (10.25).

Thousands of years later, tools still shouldn't boast. Even Apollos and Paul—men of mighty influence in the life of the early church—were simply "servants through whom you believed." Instruments of service don't exist to magnify themselves. "So neither he who plants nor he who waters is anything, but only God who gives the growth" (1 Cor 3.5–7). Preachers need to remember that Sundays are a celebration of what God has done, not a demonstration of what they can do.

In Matthew 6, Jesus encouraged all of his disciples to beware practicing their righteousness before other people in order to be seen by them, "for then you will have no reward from your Father who is in heaven." So when you give to the needy, don't sound a social media trumpet. When you pray, don't be like the hypocrite who prays for the sake of appearances. Wrenches don't sing their own praises. Mowers don't magnify themselves.

> "So you also, when you have done all that you were commanded, say, 'We are unworthy servants; we have only done what was our duty.'" (Luke 17.10)

Do what you were created to do this weekend. Fill the gaps. Meet the needs. Shine for the reputation of Jesus. And trust that the Father who sees in secret will reward you.

# SATURDAY

## *Living Letters From Jesus*

In 2 Corinthians 3.2–3, Paul and Timothy wrote to the church of God that was at Corinth:

> You yourselves are our letter of recommendation, written on our hearts, to be known and read by all. And you show that you are a letter from Christ delivered by us, written not with ink but with the Spirit of the living God, not on tablets of stone but on tablets of human hearts.

What a powerful way of thinking about a Christian's transformation and influence! The Spirit inscribes the will of the living God on our hearts so that, as we are being transformed by the gospel, we might function as "a letter from Christ" that can be read by anyone.

"Dear world, this is life the way I meant it to be…"

"Dear image-bearer, this is what your Creator desires to do in and for you…"

"Dear broken, do you see how I can pick up the pieces and reshape anyone for their good and my glory?"

"Dear lost, look at the possibilities when hope is set on things above…"

"Dear deceived, notice how you can be washed, sanctified, and justified in my name by my Spirit…"

"Dear prodigal, if your Father was willing to graciously welcome *this* wanderer home…"

"Not that we are sufficient in ourselves to claim anything as coming from us, but our sufficiency is from God" (2 Cor 3.5). Disciples of Jesus get no more credit for the good news in the "letter" than ink gets for being applied to paper.

But what a privilege and responsibility to serve as living letters from Jesus, drawing attention to the transforming power of our Father in heaven! May we serve as clear communications from our Savior to a world in need of saving today.

# WEEK TEN

## SUNDAY

### *Ever Sing. For Joy.*

"Evil may not dwell with you" (Psa 5.4). God's written revelation to mankind contains such good news of salvation, reconciliation, and even dwelling in the house of the LORD forever. But certain ugly things cannot, will not dwell with him. "For you are not a God who delights in wickedness." The boastful, evildoers, bloodthirsty, and deceitful (5.4–6) are "cast out" because of "the abundance of their transgressions" (5.9–10). Evil cannot be at home with a righteous God.

> But let all who take refuge in you rejoice;
>> let them ever sing for joy,
> and spread your protection over them,
>> that those who love your name may exult in you.
> For you bless the righteous, O LORD;
>> you cover him with favor as with a shield. (Psa 5.11–12)

Refuge. Protection. Blessing. Cover. Favor. Look at what the LORD is willing to do and be for those who love his name. It's important to notice that walking the path of righteousness does not exempt you from "groaning" at times. But even in the groaning, the righteous know where to turn. "Give ear to my words, O LORD" (5.1). Tears are shed along the path of righteousness, but they do not fall in isolation.

Give attention to the sound of my cry,
    my King and my God,
    for to you do I pray.
O LORD, in the morning you hear my voice;
    in the morning I prepare a sacrifice for you and watch (5.2–3)

Along the way, we encounter people with zero interest in dwelling with the good Father—men and women in whose mouths is no truth, whose inmost selves are full of destruction because they have rebelled against the Author of life (5.9–10).

But I, through the abundance of your steadfast love,
    will enter your house.
I will bow down toward your holy temple
    in the fear of you. (5.7)

And what do the humbly desperate experience as they walk "through the abundance" of God's steadfast love? Protection. Blessing. Cover. Favor.

Let all who take refuge in you rejoice;
    let them ever sing for joy... (Psa 5.11)

Groaning at times, yet rejoicing. Crying at times, yet ever singing. Not because circumstances are perfect, or we're consistently being treated the way we would like, or the world is at peace, or life has turned out exactly the way we planned, but because our King blesses the righteous and covers them with favor, as with a shield.

Rejoice in the Lord always; again I will say, rejoice. Let your reasonableness be known to everyone. The Lord is at hand. (Phil 4.4–5)

And so we ever sing. For joy.

# MONDAY

## *An Easily Overlooked Example Worth Imitating This Week*

You know their names. Abel. Enoch. Noah. You remember their stories. Abraham. Sarah. Isaac. Jacob. Thanks to passages like Hebrews 11 in the Bible, they endure as examples of the assurance of things hoped for, the conviction of things not seen. Millennia later, when we think of faith, we think Joseph. Moses. Samuel. David.

**But don't overlook Hananiah.** His is a name easily overlooked and long forgotten by most. This time next week, you won't remember his name in the way you remember those names in Hebrews 11. So who was Hananiah? In Nehemiah 7.1–2, recorded for all time…

> Now when the wall had been built and I had set up the doors, and the gatekeepers, the singers, and the Levites had been appointed, I gave my brother Hanani and Hananiah the governor of the castle charge over Jerusalem, for he was a more faithful and God-fearing man than many.

Hananiah didn't build an ark. He didn't cross the Red Sea as on dry land. He didn't stop the mouths of lions or receive the dead back by resurrection. He was just "a more faithful and God-fearing man than many," the sort of person Nehemiah would have desperately needed.

That's a goal you and I can wrap our minds around this week. Those are relatable footsteps we can follow. Hananiah was reliable and he feared God. In his own way, he served the purposes of God and his peers in his own generation.

God isn't asking you to deliver a message to a Pharaoh or face off with a Philistine giant or wander about for the rest of your life in deserts and mountains and caves. But he *does* expect you to be faithful, and to fear him. At work. On the road. In school. At home.

Faithful and God-fearing. You won't find Hananiah's name in Hebrews 11, but his is a name worth remembering this week. Most of all, he's an example worth imitating.

# TUESDAY

## *The Jesus of the Present Tense*

The record of human history is full of men and women who accomplished amazing things. We can study their past, analyze their actions, discuss their legacies, and express appreciation for the benefits we enjoy today because of the significant marks they left on the world. But we speak of them in the past tense, and rightfully so. They've come, impacted their era, and gone into the pages of posterity.

Scripture similarly speaks of Jesus of Nazareth in the past tense. Consider Hebrews 2 as an example and notice all of the things he accomplished.

- He "was made" lower than the angels for a little while (2.9)
- He "partook" of flesh and blood so that through death he might destroy the one who has the power of death (2.14)
- God "bore" witness to his Son by signs, wonders, and various miracles (2.4)
- A great salvation "was declared" by the Lord (2.3)
- He "was crowned" with glory and honor because of the suffering of death, so that by the grace of God he might taste death for everyone (2.9)

Jesus of Nazareth accomplished some amazing, matchless, world-changing things. In the past.

**But it's the change of tense at the end of Hebrews 2 that I'd really encourage you to think about today.**

For because he himself has suffered when tempted, *he is able* to help those who are being tempted. (2.18)

Yes, we can learn about and analyze and discuss the contributions of countless men and women from generations past, but we understand the limits of their impact. Legacies live on and ripple effects continue to be felt, but we don't think of Alexander the Great, Queen Elizabeth I, George Washington, Amelia Earhart, or even the members of our own families who have passed on as "being able"—present tense—to help us on an ordinary Tuesday.

But Jesus? Jesus is different. Jesus is truly unique. Yes, he "partook" in the past. He "was" tempted. He "bore." He "suffered." He "was" declared and "was" crowned. But in Hebrews 2 (and throughout the New Testament), we're being led to think of and speak of and share and align ourselves with the Jesus of the present tense. He "is" alive. He "is" seated at the right hand of the throne of the Majesty in heaven. He "is" able to help those who are being tempted. He always "lives" to make intercession for those who draw near to God through him.

Our Savior and King *is*—present tense—and that changes everything about our past, our today, and our future.

# WEDNESDAY

*Ancient Fuel for Today's Zeal*

*Genesis, Exodus, Leviticus, Numbers, Deuteronomy,* and *Joshua.* How would you summarize the first six books of the Bible? Having waded through the familiar and the challenging, the history and the law, what are these books really documenting and communicating? In Joshua 24, Israel's aged leader provided a summary:

- Long ago, your ancestors lived beyond the Euphrates and served other gods
- The LORD led Abraham to the land of Canaan and blessed him with a son, Isaac
- To Isaac the LORD gave Jacob
- Jacob and his children went down to Egypt
- The LORD sent Moses and Aaron, plagued Egypt, and brought Abraham's descendants out
- Against enemy after enemy, the LORD delivered Israel
- He has given you a land on which you have not labored and cities you have not built

And then, Joshua gets to the point. **"Now therefore…"** Joshua's aim in summarizing the past is to shape the hearts of the people in the present.

"Now therefore fear the LORD and serve him in sincerity and in faithfulness. Put away the gods that your fathers served beyond the River and in Egypt, and serve the LORD. And if it is evil in your eyes to serve the LORD, choose this day whom you will serve, whether the gods your fathers served in the region beyond the River, or the gods of the Amorites in whose land you dwell. But as for me and my house, we will serve the LORD." (Josh 24.14–15)

Why read and study and meditate upon the Old Testament? The past has a direct connection to the **"now."** Documented history projects a **"therefore"** into the present. Resolutions like "as for me and my house, we will serve the LORD" are great, but they need kindling and fuel, which is exactly what God has provided in the first six books of his written revelation to mankind. "This is what God has done, **now therefore**, this is what I am choosing to do."

Do you want to get serious about reverently serving God in sincerity and faithfulness? Dig deeply into the rich reservoir of ancient fuel he has preserved for the zeal of his people in the present.

# THURSDAY

## *Not "If," But "When"*

As you read the Gospels, it's remarkable how straightforwardly Jesus talks about his coming resurrection from the dead. Long before it happens, he repeatedly and very matter-of-factly talks about what **is going to happen**.

In Mark 9, for instance, after his transfiguration, on the way down the mountain with Peter, James, and John, "he charged them to tell no one what they had seen, **until the Son of Man had risen** from the dead" (Mark 9.9).

No ifs, ands, or buts. He spoke of it so plainly. "Don't tell anyone what you have seen on this high mountain **until I have risen** from the dead." Now, it would obviously be one thing to talk about what was going to happen and what others should do when it happens ... and then ... for nothing to happen. **But it did.** Jesus *did* rise from the dead, just as he so boldly foretold.

Here's something worth thinking about throughout the day: Jesus not only straightforwardly talked about his own resurrection from the dead, he repeatedly and very matter-of-factly talked about **your** resurrection.

> "Do not marvel at this, for an hour is coming when all who are in the tombs will hear his voice and come out, those who have done good to the resurrection of life, and those who have done evil to the resurrection of judgment." (John 5.28–29)

No ifs, ands, or buts. He spoke of it so plainly. Long before it happens, he repeatedly and very matter-of-factly talked about what **is going to happen**.

In light of his own empty tomb, are we listening?

One more thought to chew on from Mark 9. "Truly, I say to you, there are some standing here who will not **taste death** until they see the kingdom of God after it has come with power" (Mark 9.1). There's much we can learn from that statement, but for the moment, just reflect on those two words: **taste death**.

Death isn't the end. After death, we don't cease to exist. Each one of us will have to "taste" it—and it is a bitter, stinging taste—but death does not have the final word. Just as Jesus told his apostles what to do after he had risen from the dead, he has told us what will happen after we have tasted death ... and what to do now in order to be prepared.

In Christ, we don't have to wish upon a star. We've not been left to hang everything on an "if." Jesus straightforwardly spoke in terms of "when." "**When** the Son of Man has risen from the dead..." And he did. The same Jesus so very matter-of-factly spoke of "**when**" all who are in the tombs will come out... And we will.

Because he lives, we can face tomorrow. Because he lives, all fear is gone. He holds the future, and us, in the palm of his hand. It's not a matter of "if," it's simply a matter of "when."

# FRIDAY

## *"Paying" Attention*

2 Chronicles 33 describes the rollercoaster reign of Manasseh, king of Judah. Along the way to rock bottom, the chronicler provides this sad summary:

> Manasseh led Judah and the inhabitants of Jerusalem astray, to do more evil than the nations whom the LORD destroyed before the people of Israel. (2 Chron 33.9)

Notice what we're told in the next verse:

> "The LORD spoke to Manasseh and to his people, **but they paid no attention.**"

Attention, like money or time, is a finite resource—we only have so much to give. When we "pay" attention, we choose to give of our focus. We sacrifice other things or opportunities in order to concentrate. We watch. We listen. We take notice. On the other hand, when we "pay no attention," we're acting as if we aren't aware or as if the seeker isn't worthy of our sacrifice.

In 2 Chronicles 33, the LORD was asking for Manasseh's attention, and for good reason.

- The pivot of repentance begins with the paying of attention
- Setting my mind on things above demands the paying of attention

- The "golden rule" is practiced only by those who are paying attention
- Seeking first the kingdom of God won't happen if I'm not paying attention
- I'll never deny myself without a healthy investment of my attention

I live in a crazy-noisy world, which means now is a good time to reflect. When am I going to take a little bit of the day my Creator has provided and "pay" him what he deserves? Spending time with an open Bible will involve a little bit of sacrifice. Prayer might involve turning off a screen. Assembling this Lord's day with my brothers and sisters in Christ will take some effort. But what difference could be made in my life—and the lives of others—if I "paid" my God the attention he deserves?

"Look at the birds of the air." "Consider the lilies of the field." The Creator has been mindful of us. As we see the work of his hands in every direction—the sun, moon, and stars that he has set in place—are we paying attention?

# SATURDAY

## *The More You Know…*

> Now concerning food offered to idols: we know that "all of us possess knowledge." This "knowledge" puffs up, but love builds up. If anyone imagines that he knows something, he does not yet know as he ought to know. (1 Cor 8.1–2)

Here's something worth thinking about this weekend: the more you know, the more you ought to love.

Unfortunately, that's not always true. Sometimes, the more we know, the more impressed we become with ourselves. Sometimes, the more we know, the less we think of others. Sometimes, the more we know, the more "puffed up" we get.

Notice how the Holy Spirit describes this sort of "knowing." If anyone "imagines that he knows something, he does not yet know as he ought to know." In other words, the real aim of knowing has been neglected or forgotten and my learning has led me to the land of self-centered imagination.

In 1 Corinthians 8.6 we're reminded, "there is one God, the Father, from whom are all things and for whom we exist." Think about that. I exist from God, for God. What amount of "knowledge" could I possibly acquire that would merit shifting attention away from him to myself? It's not about me. When *I* allow *myself* to become so impressed with *myself* that *I* get "puffed up," I'm missing the point of my very existence.

But when I remember, "I exist from God, for God," now I have a different focus. A better ambition. **Love**. The love that glorifies my Creator. The love that builds other image-bearers up. The love that sacrifices as my Savior has sacrificed.

If "the fear of the LORD is the beginning of knowledge" (Prov 1.7), isn't love the aim of knowledge?

The more I know, the more I ought to love.

# WEEK ELEVEN

## SUNDAY

### *Don't Clog God's Blessings*

You don't have to be perfect in order to be blessed by God. Just listen to the beginning of Psalm 32: "Blessed is the one whose transgression is forgiven, whose sin is covered." Our Creator is a gracious fountain of amazing blessings to undeserving people.

But Psalm 32 also calls us to consistently look inward. "Blessed is the man... in whose spirit there is no deceit" (32.2). If God is the fountain, deceit is the clog that can lodge in our spirits and block the full enjoyment of his blessings. A clog in a water drain is annoying. A clog in a heart artery is dangerous. A clog in our spirits can cause us to miss out on God's blessings in the present and cost us our souls in eternity.

Listen to David's description of how it feels when we ignore our consciences and comfortably settle with deceit. "When I kept silent, my bones wasted away... For day and night your hand was heavy upon me; my strength was dried up" (32.3–4). But, when "I acknowledged my sin to you, and I did not cover my iniquity, I said, 'I will confess my transgressions to the LORD,' and you forgave my sin" (32.5).

Deceit in the spirit—a stubborn unwillingness to be honest— is the nasty obstruction that will limit the flow of God's amazing grace in our lives. "Therefore let everyone who is godly offer prayer to you at a time when you may be found" (32.6). Listen to those words. God *wants* to be found, and when he is, the finder is never disappointed. "Steadfast love surrounds the one who trusts in the Lord" (32.10).

The question, then, is simple: Do you trust him? Do you trust him enough to be honest? To acknowledge your sin? To ask for help? To be surrounded by his steadfast love and transformed by his grace?

Blessed indeed is the person in whose spirit there is no deceit.

# MONDAY

## *Can It Bear Your Weight?*

"On what do you rest this trust of yours?" (2 Kings 18.19)

It came from the trash-talking spokesman of a pagan king, but it was a good question. "Say to Hezekiah, 'Thus says the great king, the king of Assyria: On what do you rest this trust of yours?'"

Trust that "rests on" someone or something... that's an image worth chewing on today.

In Hezekiah's day, to trust in Egypt could be compared to resting your hand and putting your weight on a broken reed—it "will pierce the hand of any man who leans on it" (2 Kings 18.21). While that's an image that makes most of us cringe, we can readily understand the point: some things shouldn't be leaned upon. *Most* things, in fact, were never intended to bear the weight we humans frequently place upon them. Which means, "On what do you rest this trust of yours?" continues to be a great question.

Money was never intended to bear the weight of your trust. Notice: "The love of money is a root of all kinds of evils. It is through this craving that some have wandered away from the faith and *pierced* themselves with many pangs" (1 Tim 6.10). Rest your trust on money and it will pierce you.

Work was never intended to bear the weight of your identity. Rest your identity on your career and it will pierce you.

Marriage was never intended to bear the weight of your joy. Rest the deepest needs of your heart on your spouse and you'll both get hurt.

Children were never intended to bear the weight of your hope. Resting your hopes and dreams on your kids is a recipe for disaster.

You were never intended to bear the weight of the world, but if you act like it revolves around you, it will crush you.

The church was never intended to rest on you as its cornerstone…

You get the idea.

So, "On what do you rest this trust of yours?" Great question. No *thing* is sufficient. Only One is.

> The LORD is my rock and my fortress and my deliverer,
>> my God, my rock, in whom I take refuge,
>> my shield, and the horn of my salvation, my stronghold.
> (Psa 18.2)

In a world of good things that will pierce anyone who puts too much weight on them, Jesus allowed himself to be pierced so that we could build and rest the full weight of our lives on solid rock.

> What have I to dread, what have I to fear,
> Leaning on the everlasting arms?
> I have blessed peace with my Lord so near,
> Leaning on the everlasting arms. (Elisha A. Hoffman, 1887)

Trust him. Lean on him today. He alone can bear your weight.

# TUESDAY

## *Remind Them…*

Whether we live in the first or the twenty-first century, we inhabit a world which lies under the sway of the evil one. Day by day, we witness and experience some ugly things. Foolishness. Disobedience. Deception. Slavery to passions and pleasures. Malice. Envy. Hatred. We know this because we are more than witnesses to the ugliness; we've been participants.

> For we ourselves were once foolish, disobedient, led astray, slaves to various passions and pleasures, passing our days in malice and envy, hated by others and hating one another. (Titus 3.3)

But something has changed. More accurately, Someone has changed us.

> But when the goodness and loving kindness of God our Savior appeared, he saved us, not because of works done by us in righteousness, but according to his own mercy, by the washing of regeneration and renewal of the Holy Spirit, whom he poured out on us richly through Jesus Christ our Savior, so that being justified by his grace we might become heirs according to the hope of eternal life. (Titus 3.4–7)

We are hope-filled heirs of the gracious, conquering King. And yet, we continue to witness and experience a world that lies under the sway of the evil one for a little while longer. So how should we conduct ourselves in the midst of such darkness? "Remind them," the apostle Paul charges Titus. Remind those disciples living on the island of Crete, a haven of "liars, evil beasts, and lazy gluttons" (1.12).

> Remind them to be submissive to rulers and authorities, to be obedient, to be ready for every good work, to speak evil of no one, to avoid quarreling, to be gentle, and to show perfect courtesy toward all people. (3.1–2)

This is what it looks like to be the salt of the earth. Not foolish and disobedient, but submissive. Not deceiving, but ready for every good work. Not slaves to various passions and pleasures, but resolved to speak evil of no one. Not passing our days in malice or envy, but taking a pass on ever-present opportunities to quarrel. Not full of hatred, but gentle, demonstrating perfect courtesy toward all people.

First century Crete needed light. So does twenty-first century America. In Titus 3, we've just been reminded where the light comes from.

# WEDNESDAY

## *"We Don't Have Enough"*

**"We don't have enough."** This, I'm afraid, is how most of us think. I know it's the direction *my* mind most naturally goes. We don't have enough ...

> People. Resources. Volunteers. Opportunities. Square footage. Experience. Expertise. Influence.

... therefore it won't work. And if it *does* work, it's easy for us mere mortals to take the credit because somehow *we* made it work.

But God doesn't think like us. In fact, at the very moment we're saying, "We don't have enough," he very well may be saying, "You have too many."

Israel faced impossible odds in the days of Gideon. The Midianites and the Amalekites and all the people of the East had encamped against them "like locusts in abundance, and their camels were without number, as the sand that is on the seashore in abundance" (Judges 7.12).

So the Lord said to Gideon:

> "The people with you are too many for me to give the Midianites into their hand, lest Israel boast over me, saying, 'My own hand has saved me.'" (7.2)

So God whittles Gideon's army down from 32,000 to 10,000 to 300.

And the LORD said to Gideon, "With the 300 men who lapped I will save you and give the Midianites into your hand." (7.7)

Did you catch that? **I** will save you. **I** will give the horde into your hand. And when I do, Israel will have no reason to boast, "My own hand has saved me."

The Bible is full of the testimonies…

- "We're not enough." But God is.
- "I'm not strong enough." But God is.
- "I'm not good enough." But God is.
- "I don't know enough." But God does.

Maybe, while we're lamenting the fact that "We don't have enough" in hearts that are far too eager to draw attention to and boast in ourselves, God is saying, "You have too many," and waiting for us to practice what we preach.

# THURSDAY

## *Securing the Gate of Your Heart*

...so that Satan may not tempt you because of your lack of self-control. (1 Cor 7.5)

Your one and only God-given heart is the most precious territory of your existence. From it flow the "springs of life" (Prov 4.23). This precious territory needs to be guarded with vigilance. When passions are at war *within* our hearts, we quarrel and fight with others (James 4.1). When desires are lured from *without* and our affections give chase to temptation, sin is born within (James 1.14–15).

It should be no surprise, then, that **self-control** is a frequent prescription for disciples of Jesus. Self-control is a fruit of the Spirit (Gal 5.22), a goal of our training in grace (Titus 2.11–12), and a vital supplement for our spiritual health (2 Pet 1.5–6). In its absence, the gateway of the heart is left open to temptation. Without it, we are giving the devil an opportunity (Eph 4.26–27).

In 1 Corinthians 7.37, the apostle Paul provides priceless details for the one who is looking to take this spiritual struggle seriously:

- A **"determination"** must be made: only One has the rightful authority to reign on the throne of my heart; I'm not him and neither is the devil
- Desire must be brought **"under control"**; this is the will of my true and rightful King (1 Thes 4.3–5)

- By his grace, with the strength that God supplies, I can be **"firmly established"** in heart, equipped and alert to "keep" it "with all vigilance"

Your one and only God-given heart is the most precious territory of your existence. What will you do this week to secure it, guard it, and use it as a platform from which to glorify God as your Savior and Lord?

# FRIDAY

## *Do You Do Well to Be Angry?*

In Jonah 4.4, God asked Jonah a simple question:

"Do you do well to be angry?"

Anyone and everyone can get angry. That's not challenging at all. But *when* I'm angry, am I doing *well* to be angry? That's the challenging question of my Creator.

> Therefore, having put away falsehood, let each one of you speak the truth with his neighbor, for we are members one of another. Be angry and do not sin; do not let the sun go down on your anger, and give no opportunity to the devil. (Eph 4.25–27)

The devil doesn't care if you're angry with the right person, with the right motive, to the right degree, for the right amount of time, but your Father in heaven *does* care. When unbridled anger is allowed to flare at the wrong person, with the wrong motive, to the wrong degree, for the wrong amount of time, the devil delights. God grieves.

Not *if*, but *when* you feel the fuel of anger igniting in your heart, remember the simple question asked Jonah:

"Do you do well to be angry?"

Honestly asking that question could keep the devil away from a foothold in your heart and present your heavenly Father with an opportunity to shape you for the better.

> Whoever is slow to anger is better than the mighty,
>> and he who rules his spirit than he who takes a city.
>> (Prov 16.32)

# SATURDAY

## *When You Love Jesus, Expect Company*

One of my goals for today is to meditate on one verse from the Bible—to turn it over in my head throughout the day and allow each phrase to sink into the recesses of my heart. I invite you to do the same. Remember and reflect on this one verse. I've written it down on a little piece of paper and stuck it in my pocket. I plan on coming back to it again and again as the day unfolds. It's God-breathed fuel for my journey home. Ready? Here it is:

> "If anyone loves me, he will keep my word, and my Father will love him, and we will come to him and make our home with him." (John 14.23)

**To love Jesus is to open the gate of my heart,** recognizing the sovereignty of my true and rightful King. His word is to be treasured. If I truly love him, his word will take root in my heart and bear the fruit of obedience.

**To love Jesus is to *be* loved by the Father.** God is love. By this we know love, that his Son laid down his life for us. When I humble myself under the mighty hand of the Son, I am the heir of a divine promise: the Father not only loves the Son; he loves me.

**To love Jesus is to have company.** Listen to the Lord on the night of his betrayal: "We will come to him and make our home with him." As John would remind in his first letter, "God is love, and whoever abides in love abides in God, and God abides in him" (1 John 4.16).

Do you love Jesus? If so, you will keep his word. You will *be* loved. You should expect company. And you can rest assured, "I am heaven-bound."

> Let what you heard from the beginning abide in you. If what you heard from the beginning abides in you, then you too will abide in the Son and in the Father. And this is the promise that he made to us—eternal life. (1 John 2.24–25)

# WEEK TWELVE

## SUNDAY

### *Study. Appreciate. Delight.*

"Great are the works of the Lord, studied by all who delight in them." (Psa 111.2)

Our Creator has preserved an incredible written revelation of his "great works." The more we study the Bible, the more we will be able to say, "Now I see." And the more we see, the more reasons we will find to "delight" in the One who has been so good to us. With "whole hearts" (Psa 111.1) let's say with the psalmist today:

- Praise the Lord! I give thanks to him (111.1)
- His work is full of splendor and majesty (111.3)
- His righteousness endures forever (111.3)
- He is gracious and merciful (111.4)
- He remembers his covenant forever (111.5)
- The works of his hands are faithful and just (111.7)
- His precepts are trustworthy (111.7)
- Holy and awesome is his name! (111.9)
- Fearing him is the first step on the path to wisdom (111.10)
- Walking in his wisdom gives me good understanding (111.10)
- The singing of his praise will continue today through me (111.10)

Could I ask a personal question? **How full of delight has your heart been this past week?** Are you suffering from a lack of gratitude? Does God seem distant? Are you struggling to hope? Have you been walking in selfish shortsightedness? Stumbling through life without meaning or purpose? Do you feel lost? Trying wrong path after wrong path, are you delight-starved?

Maybe the author of Psalm 111 knows what he's talking about. "Great are the works of the LORD, studied by all who delight in them." Let's study, appreciate, and thank God today for his awesome accomplishments. Beyond today, let's use our study and worship as fuel for delight in God this week.

# MONDAY

## *As Truth Continues to Stumble...*

How long ago would you guess these words were written?

> Justice is turned back,
>> and righteousness stands far away;
> for truth has stumbled in the public squares,
>> and uprightness cannot enter.
> Truth is lacking,
>> and he who departs from evil makes himself a prey.

The answer? **Two thousand, seven hundred years ago** in Isaiah 59.14–15. Think about that. Words that could be written today to describe some of humanity's most grievous ongoing problems are more than twenty-seven centuries old. And we can't blame our Creator.

> Behold, the Lord's hand is not shortened, that it cannot save,
>> or his ear dull, that it cannot hear;
> but your iniquities have made a separation
>> between you and your God,
> and your sins have hidden his face from you
>> so that he does not hear. (Isa 59.1–2)

The result of the separation? Devastating.

> ...our sins testify against us;
> for our transgressions are with us,
>> and we know our iniquities:

transgressing, and denying the LORD,
    and turning back from following our God,
speaking oppression and revolt,
    conceiving and uttering from the heart lying words.
(59.12–13)

Not great news to share on a Monday, is it? But listen. The good news greater than the bad in this section of Isaiah's prophecy is that "a Redeemer will come" (59.20).

> "As for me, this is my covenant with them," says the LORD: "My Spirit that is upon you, and my words that I have put in your mouth, shall not depart out of your mouth, or out of the mouth of your offspring, or out of the mouth of your children's offspring," says the LORD, "from this time forth and forevermore." (59.21)

Justice continues to be turned back in the kingdoms of this world. Righteousness often stands far away. Truth still stumbles in the public squares of humanity. **But our Redeemer has come.** What news needs more sharing this week than that? Let's live as his covenant people today. May the words of our mouths and the meditations of our hearts be acceptable in his sight above all. May the people still dwelling in a land of deep darkness see something different—something better—reflected in us.

A great light.

# TUESDAY

## *Love Comes to Life*

No one has ever seen God; if we love one another, God abides in us and his love is perfected in us. (1 John 4.12)

"Beloved." Six times John uses that word to address his reader. "Beloved." You are loved. In fact, "love is from God, and whoever loves has been born of God and knows God. Anyone who does not love does not know God, because God is love" (4.7–8).

And where does God's love come most sharply into focus? "God sent his only Son into the world, so that we might live through him. In this is love, not that we have loved God but that he loved us and sent his Son to be the propitiation for our sins" (4.9–10).

"Beloved," this ought to change our lives. "If God so loved us, we also ought to love one another" (4.11). And notice, meditate on the potential behind the "ought." "No one has ever seen God; if we love one another, God abides in us and his love is perfected in us" (4.12).

Amazing. What we've just been told is **amazing**. God *is* love and when we love, the influence of the One who has never been seen *can* be seen in fleshy, tangible, relatable ways.

When we are patient and kind, we are reflectors of otherworldly light.

When we stop insisting on our own way—leaving rudeness, arrogance, envy, and resentment behind—the darkness is forced to forfeit a little more of its territory.

When we bear all things, believe all things, hope all things, and endure all things in the name of the One who *is* love, the unseen God abides in us. More than that, his love is perfected in us. Even more than that, the influence of the Invisible comes to be on full display for those who do not know God. Love comes to life.

So we have come to know and to believe the love that God has for us. God is love, and whoever abides in love abides in God, and God abides in him. (4.16)

The invisible made visible. At home. At work. At school. At the restaurant. In the neighborhood. Christians believe the love. We know the love. We abide in the love. **And we're to be living representations of the love**.

Love in the flesh. That's Jesus. Love come to life. That's the calling of his "beloved."

# WEDNESDAY

## *The Darkening Effect of Words Without Knowledge*

Then the LORD answered Job out of the whirlwind and said:

"Who is this that darkens counsel by words without knowledge?
Dress for action like a man;
  I will question you, and you make it known to me."
(Job 38.1–3)

"Answer" shows up 66 times in the Old Testament book of *Job*. Why did those terrible things happen to Job and his family? What did Job do to deserve it all? What sort of sin must he be hiding? Where was God then? Where is he now? Chapter after chapter, everyone is looking for answers.

After 35 chapters of speculation, accusation, and debate, the LORD finally answers. We would do well to meditate on his first question. "Who is this that darkens counsel by words without knowledge?"

**Words.** It's never been easier to broadcast them, far and wide—spoken words, written words, recorded words, even livestreamed words. But the easier it is to share, the more care we ought to take. "When words are many, transgression is not lacking, but whoever restrains his lips is prudent" (Prov 10.19).

**Without knowledge.** What good is an abundance of words without knowledge as the foundation? "A fool takes no pleasure in understanding, but only in expressing his opinion" (Prov 18.2). We need to be so very careful when it comes to speculating, accusing, and debating things we actually know little about. "Do you see a man who is hasty in his words?" That's the reckless path of the fool (Prov 29.20).

**Darkens counsel.** Careless words have a devious tendency (at least for a time) to obscure the truth. Sensational lies are easy to believe and alluring to spread. Foolishness is fun in the moment. Wise counsel that cautions and restrains doesn't seem as thrilling as reckless abandonment. "You do you" costs much less than "Be made new." But the wisdom of Proverbs 6.23 continues to tell us the truth. "The commandment is a lamp and the teaching a light, and the reproofs of discipline are the way of life."

Some things are hidden from us by divine design, undoubtedly for our good. There are secret things that belong only to God. May we be humble enough to accept that fact. May we hear the Lord's "Where were you?" questions in Job 38 and be put in our place, even in the 21st century.

In the meantime, as disciples of Jesus, may our words reflect the Light of the world. May they be governed by fear of the Lord, which is the beginning of knowledge. May they be shaped by truth, fueled by love, and grace-giving to the people around us.

# THURSDAY

## *Remember What Matters to Jesus*

And as [Jesus] came out of the temple, one of his disciples said to him, "Look, Teacher, what wonderful stones and what wonderful buildings!" And Jesus said to him, "Do you see these great buildings? There will not be left here one stone upon another that will not be thrown down." (Mark 13.1–2)

The temple of Jesus' day was a physical wonder to behold, no doubt. But what should have been a house of prayer had been transformed into a den of robbers. The jewel of Jerusalem had been corrupted into a centerpiece of greed, self-indulgence, lawlessness, and hypocrisy—a beautiful, gigantic white-washed tomb.

Isn't there a principle here worth thinking about throughout the day? **The LORD sees not as man sees.** How many times has God shown it throughout human history? How many ways has he documented that fact in his revelation to mankind? The LORD sees not as man sees. We are far too easily impressed with the outward appearance, but the LORD looks on the heart. Which means...

You may live in a wonderful house with wonderful furnishings, but what really matters is that God is the rock upon which your home is being built.

You may assemble on Sundays in a wonderful building with wonderful conveniences, but what really matters is that you worship in spirit and truth.

You may work for a wonderful company that makes wonderful profits, but what really matters is that you are serving the Lord Christ.

You may raise wonderfully successful children who are wonderfully applauded for their secular accomplishments, but what really matters is that they grow to walk with Jesus.

You may live in a wonderful country of wonderful freedoms, but what really matters is that your citizenship is in heaven.

You may go on wonderful vacations to wonderful destinations, but what really matters is whether or not you are heaven-bound.

"Look, Teacher, what wonderful stones and what wonderful buildings!" What impresses Jesus is wonderful faith.

Let's remember to keep the main thing the main thing today.

# FRIDAY

## *What's an Ebenezer?*

**"Here I raise my Ebenezer; hither by Thy help I've come."** Have you ever sung those words and had *no idea* what you were singing? If so, you're not the first. What in the world is an "Ebenezer"? What does it have to do with God's help? And if I don't even know what an Ebenezer is, how can I raise one?

Before you sing *O Thou Fount of Every Blessing* again, you should spend a little time in 1 Samuel 7. Samuel has become a leader in Israel and called the people to repentance.

> "If you are returning to the LORD with all your heart, then put away the foreign gods and the Ashtaroth from among you and direct your heart to the LORD and serve him only, and he will deliver you out of the hand of the Philistines." So the people of Israel put away the Baals and the Ashtaroth, and they served the LORD only. (7.3–4)

Samuel gathers the people in a place called Mizpah that he might pray for them. They fast on a day of sacrifice and confess, "We have sinned against the LORD."

> Now when the Philistines heard that the people of Israel had gathered at Mizpah, the lords of the Philistines went up against Israel. And when the people of Israel heard of it, they were afraid of the Philistines. (7.7)

They desperately implore Samuel, "Do not cease to cry out to the LORD our God for us, that he may save us from the hand of the Philistines." Samuel offers a sacrifice and "cries out" to the LORD for Israel. "And the LORD answered him."

> As Samuel was offering up the burnt offering, the Philistines drew near to attack Israel. But the LORD thundered with a mighty sound that day against the Philistines and threw them into confusion, and they were defeated before Israel. (7.10)

There could be no doubt on that day as to the identity of Israel's deliverer. So Samuel took a stone, set it up, and called its name Ebenezer; "for he said, 'Till now the LORD has helped us'" (7.12). *Ebenezer* means "stone of help."

**"Here I raise my Ebenezer; hither by Thy help I've come."** It's a beautiful way of expressing to God, "I've only made it this far because you have been with me. I thank you for being my Stone of help. I praise you as the Fount of my blessings. I will continue to depend upon you, every step of the way."

Till now the LORD has helped us. May we humbly recognize that fact and live today with joyful dependence on him.

# SATURDAY

## *Though You Do Not Now See Him...*

**"You have not seen him."** That's the reality we live with as modern disciples. Does that leave us at a severe disadvantage? Have we been separated by just too many centuries? We've never laid our physical eyes on Jesus, never touched him with our hands or heard him with our ears. But this fact isn't ignored or glossed over in Scripture, and it's certainly not presented as an obstacle to faith or an insurmountable barrier to joy. Just listen to what the apostle Peter—who *had* seen and heard and touched Jesus—wrote to people of his own era.

> Though you have not seen him, you love him. Though you do not now see him, you believe in him and rejoice with joy that is inexpressible and filled with glory, obtaining the outcome of your faith, the salvation of your souls. (1 Pet 1.8–9)

Think about that. Many, many people who lived in the first century never laid eyes on Jesus. And yet, they could be "born again to a living hope" through Jesus' resurrection from the dead (1.3).

The vast majority of people who lived in the first century never heard Jesus speak. And yet, they could be confident of "an inheritance that is imperishable, undefiled, and unfading, kept in heaven" for them (1.4).

Men and women who had been dispersed throughout Pontus, Galatia, Cappadocia, Asia, and Bithynia never had the opportunity to touch Jesus, but according to Peter himself, they were "being guarded through faith for a salvation ready to be revealed in the last time" (1.5).

And "in this you rejoice" (1.6). You've not been forgotten, abandoned, or left behind. Whether you live in the first or the eleventh or the twenty-first century, *your* hope can be set "fully on the grace that will be brought to *you* at the revelation of Jesus Christ" (1.13). Take the time to read 1 Peter 1 today and see for yourself. Souls can be purified by obedience to the truth. Sincere brotherly love can flow from purified hearts. Anyone can be born again through the living and abiding word of God. Grace is real. Hope is alive. Joy inexpressible can carry you through fiery trials. Faith in Christ still has a glorious outcome.

The elect exiles who received Peter's first letter never laid eyes on Jesus. And yet, "grace and peace" was being "multiplied" to them (1.2). They never heard Jesus preach a sermon, but their lives had been forever changed by "the good news that was preached" to them (1.25). Twenty centuries later, all flesh is still comparable to grass and all our glory like the flower of grass. The grass continues to wither. The flower continues to fall. But two thousand years have not eroded this glory-filled fact: "the word of the Lord remains forever."

Though you have not seen him, you are at no disadvantage whatsoever. Though you do not now see him, you will.

# WEEK THIRTEEN

## SUNDAY

### *For God Alone. My Soul. Waits.*

In Psalm 62.1–2, David wrote:

> For God alone my soul waits in silence;
>> from him comes my salvation.
> He alone is my rock and my salvation,
>> my fortress; I shall not be greatly shaken.

Could I encourage you to think deeply about Psalm 62.1 this week? This would be a great verse to memorize today. Write it on some Post-It notes and stick them in strategic places where you're sure to see them. Recite this verse off-and-on throughout the week. Use it as fuel for your prayers.

*For God alone my soul waits in silence...*

**"For God alone."** Remember this week that "in him (you) live and move and have (your) being" (Acts 17.28). He created you. He is sustaining you. He upholds your universe by the word of his power (Heb 1.3). Heaven is his throne and the earth is his footstool (Isa 66.1). As the heavens are higher than the earth, so are his ways higher than your ways and his thoughts than your thoughts (Isa 55.9). And yet, he desires a close, personal relationship with you. He continues to invite you to taste and see that he is good (Psa 34.8). He is worthy of your worship today and your faithful service this week. "For God alone." He's in a class all by himself.

**"My soul."** You are more than a body. There is a very real part of you created in God's own image. If he wills, this week will be full of responsibilities and opportunities—work, school, chores, projects, progress—but right now is a good moment to resolve that in the midst of the busyness, you won't neglect your soul. The day will come when the dust returns to the earth as it was, and your spirit will return to the God who gave it (Eccl 12.7). The fool wastes his or her life by focusing on the vanities of the temporary. How terrible it would be to hear from God when my time on earth is done, "You fool! This very night your soul is required of you. And now, all of those toys and trinkets you devoted so much time to, whose will they be?" So is the one who builds his life on the sand, laying up treasure for himself, all while neglecting his one and only soul.

**"Waits in silence."** You live in a noisy world. You're starting a new week that will likely be filled with dings, chimes, rings, and all sorts of racket. Let's allow our worship today to set a tone for the week. Take a little bit of time—*quiet* time—each day to commune with your Father in heaven "who sees in secret" (Matt 6.6). Pray to him. Meet him in his word. Sing his praises. Express your gratitude. Meditate on his testimonies. Ask for wisdom. Seek his face. Such quiet time very well may require unplugging, turning off, possibly even some purging. But isn't your soul worth it? Isn't your Father worthy?

**"For God alone my soul waits in silence."** Don't waste your week. Lean on Psalm 62.1 and come what may, you will not be greatly shaken.

# MONDAY

## *Don't Lose Sight of the Who*

When the what and the when and the how and the why is unclear, don't lose sight of the who.

2 Chronicles 20 describes the Moabites, Ammonites, and Meunites coming against King Jehoshaphat and Judah for battle. "Then Jehoshaphat was afraid and set his face to seek the LORD" (20.3). In a great assembly of his people, the king stands and readily confesses in prayer to God: "We are powerless against this great horde that is coming against us. We do not know what to do, but our eyes are on you" (20.12).

What a powerful example! When the what and the when and the how and the why is unclear, don't lose sight of the who.

"I have no idea what life is going to look like after school and I don't know what to do, but my eyes are on you."

"Everyone thinks I'm stronger than I feel and I don't know what to do, but my eyes are on you."

"Life hasn't turned out the way I thought it was going to and I don't know what to do, but my eyes are on you."

"I just got that call from the doctor that no one wants and I don't know what to do, but my eyes are on you."

"For the first time in decades I'm living in this house alone and I don't know what to do, but my eyes are on you."

When the what and the when and the how and the why is unclear, focus on the who. His steadfast love endures forever (2 Chron 20.21).

# TUESDAY

## *Why God Wants to Turn You*

"God, having raised up his servant, sent him to you first, to … by turning every one of you from your wickedness."

That's how Acts 3 in our Bibles ends. Almost. Two words are missing in the middle of that quote above.

First, let's come face-to-face with the fact that God wants to "turn" every one of us. The Bible word for that turning is "repentance." My Creator wants to turn me *from* my wickedness *to* the glory of his resurrected Son.

**But why?** God raised up Jesus, sent him to the first eyewitnesses, and has expressed his desire to turn every one of us from our wickedness… **WHY?**

- Not to consume me with his wrath
- Not to taunt or shame me
- Not to rain on my parade
- Not to withhold the best from me
- Not to keep me under his thumb
- Not to control me like a mindless robot
- Not to mislead me
- Not to suck all the fun out of my life

"God, having raised up his servant, sent him to you first, to **bless you** by turning every one of you from your wickedness."

Your heavenly Father didn't have to provide a sacrifice for your sins. He didn't have to extend the gospel as his power for your salvation. He didn't have to define the boundaries, warn you of the dangers, and give you time to turn.

But he did, because he wants to bless you.

It's not overbearing or mean or intrusive or rude, therefore, for him to proclaim, "Repent and turn back, that your sins may be blotted out, that times of refreshing may come from the presence of the Lord" (Acts 3.19–20).

Listen to that. He *wants* to blot out your sins. He *wants* to refresh you. He *wants* you to enjoy his presence. He *wants* to bless you.

All that stands in the way of most of us... is us.

# WEDNESDAY

### *Flickers of Faith in the Dark*

Reading the Old Testament book of *Job* is kind of like walking through a long, dark cave. If you've read the book before, you know that God will make his presence powerfully known in the last few chapters, but it's a long reading-trek to get there.

As you eavesdrop on the conversation between Job, Eliphaz, Bildad, and Zophar, you might feel like you're just being led downhill, deeper and deeper into the cave. Why has tragedy turned Job's world upside down? What did he or his family ever do to deserve this? And where is God?

Maybe, as you make your way through this long, winding cave with Job and his friends, you feel like giving up. It's a difficult book to read. Why continue to wade through the dark waters of confusion, accusation, and despair? Is reading the Bible altogether even worth it?

But every once in a while, even in that long, dark cave, you catch a flicker of light. Listen…

> "Behold, I go forward, but [God] is not there,
> and backward, but I do not perceive him;
> on the left hand when he is working, I do not behold him;
> he turns to the right hand, but I do not see him.
> But he knows the way that I take;
> when he has tried me, I shall come out as gold.

My foot has held fast to his steps;
　　I have kept his way and have not turned aside.
I have not departed from the commandment of his lips;
　　I have treasured the words of his mouth more than my
portion of food." (23.8–12)

...flickers of faith in the darkest dark Job could never have imagined.

I can't see God right now, but he knows exactly where I am. Life is hard. Very, very hard, and I don't know why. How long will this trial last? I don't know.

In the meantime, I'll follow in his footsteps. I'll stay on the path of righteousness. I won't walk away from his commandments. I'll treasure his word in my heart and depend on it more than my body depends on food.

And on the other side of this trial? **I will come out as gold.**

Count it all joy, my brothers and sisters, when you meet trials of various kinds, for you know that the testing of your faith produces steadfastness. And let steadfastness have its full effect, that you may be perfect and complete, lacking in nothing. (James 1.2–4)

Blessed is the man who remains steadfast under trial, for when he has stood the test he will receive the crown of life, which God has promised to those who love him. (James 1.12)

I do not see him. But he knows exactly where I am. The way is hard and the darkness is heavy, but when he has tried me, I will come out as gold. For he has promised, and I believe.

There are glimmers of light, even in the darkest, most difficult-to-read books of the Bible. Don't give up on reading them. The God who inspired them hasn't given up on you, and he can use them, even today, to help you see.

# THURSDAY

## *"If You Knew"*

A woman from Samaria came to draw water. Jesus said to her, "Give me a drink." (For his disciples had gone away into the city to buy food.) The Samaritan woman said to him, "How is it that you, a Jew, ask for a drink from me, a woman of Samaria?" (For Jews have no dealings with Samaritans.) Jesus answered her, "If you knew the gift of God, and who it is that is saying to you, "Give me a drink," you would have asked him, and he would have given you living water." (John 4.7–10)

**If she knew...**

If she knew that the man who was asking for a drink was in the beginning with God...

If she knew that this was the Word through whom all things were made...

If she knew the glory become flesh sitting beside that well— glory as of the only Son from the Father, full of grace and truth...

Having had five husbands, now living with a man who wasn't her husband, if she knew the gift of God...

If she knew who it was that was saying to her, "Give me a drink"...

**...she would have asked.** And then? He would have given her living water that could become within her a spring welling up to eternal life (John 4.14).

"If you knew, you would ask, and I would give." What a powerful thought, worth reflecting upon throughout the day. If I knew, I would ask, and he would give. That sounds a lot like the invitation in James 1.5.

> If any of you lacks wisdom, let him ask God, who gives generously to all without reproach, and it will be given him.

What am I lacking because I have not asked? What am I failing to ask because my eyes are not yet fully open to his glory? If I knew the gift of God and who it is that has already given himself for me, how would I live today?

Wouldn't I cast all my anxieties on him? Wouldn't I pray as if he really is able to do far more abundantly beyond all that I ask or think? Wouldn't I walk humbly with him? Wouldn't I do righteousness and justice? Wouldn't I treat my fellow image-bearers with dignity and respect? Wouldn't I love kindness? Wouldn't I practice self-control? Wouldn't I keep his commandments? Wouldn't I show the thirsty where I've found the living water? Wouldn't I live like he's coming again? Wouldn't the greatest desire of my heart be "Amen. Come, Lord Jesus"?

If I knew the One who taught in his most famous sermon…

> "Ask, and it will be given to you; seek, and you will find; knock, and it will be opened to you. For everyone who asks receives, and the one who seeks finds, and to the one who knocks it will be opened. Or which one of you, if his son asks him for bread, will give him a stone? Or if he asks for a fish, will give him a serpent? If you then, who are evil, know how to give good gifts to your children, how much more will your Father who is in heaven give good things to those who ask him!" (Matt 7.7–11)

…wouldn't I ask? And wouldn't he give?

Let's live like we know that same Jesus today.

# FRIDAY

## *Consider the Source*

Ezekiel 13 documents a fundamental problem that plagued people thousands of years ago and continues to be a dangerous pitfall.

> "Son of man, prophesy against the prophets of Israel, who are prophesying, and say to those who prophesy from their own hearts: 'Hear the word of the LORD!'" (13.2)

Did you catch the problem? At a crucial point in Israel's history, some were teaching, reassuring, and encouraging the people "from their own hearts." Their guide was "their own spirit" (13.3). They were saying, "Declares the LORD," when the LORD hadn't sent them (13.6). They were proclaiming, "Peace," when there was no peace and "smearing" fractures that desperately needed corrective attention "with whitewash" (13.10).

It doesn't take an architect or engineer to know that you can smear spackle and paint all over a crumbling wall, but "whitewash" isn't going to keep it from falling if the foundation is compromised.

These "prophets" were so convincing and deluded, they "expected" the LORD to "fulfill their word" (13.6), even though the source of their message was their own hearts. And the impact on the people around them? Devastating.

> "They have misled my people…" (13.10)

"...you have disheartened the righteous falsely, although I have not grieved him, and you have encouraged the wicked, that he should not turn from his evil way to save his life..." (13.22)

Notice especially that last verse. What good comes from "encouraging" someone who is headed away from God if traveling that path costs them their life and possibly their soul for eternity? When God is calling someone to turn in order to save them, I shouldn't be cheering them on in the wrong direction.

For millennia there have been messengers willing to tell us what we want to hear, but passages like Ezekiel 13 remind us to consider the source. Is what I'm hearing from the heart of God or the hearts of humans? If I follow the leading of this message, am I tracking with the spirit of the mere messenger or the Spirit of God?

Not all input is equally valid or valuable. Expecting the Almighty to fulfill my word is foolish. I was warned a long time ago that "the heart is deceitful above all things" (Jer 17.9). I would do well, with all that I hear, to consider the source.

# SATURDAY

*Former Things*

**Pain. Fear. Grief. Death.** They rank among the most difficult of present things.

The revelation of Jesus Christ to John describes many dark and difficult realities. However difficult they are for us to *read*, most of us can only imagine how difficult they were for a first and second-century audience to endure.

- The devil had thrown saints from Smyrna into prison (2.10)
- Antipas, a faithful witness of Jesus, had been killed among saints in Pergamum (2.13)
- Peace was taken from the earth (6.4)
- Men and women were slain for the word of God (6.9)
- Witnesses of God had been killed and their bodies left in the street (11)
- The devil, full of great wrath, had made war on those who held to the testimony of Jesus (12)
- The endurance of the saints had been tested by governmental and religious "beasts" (13)
- The "mother of earth's abominations" had become drunk with the blood of the saints (17)

Again, it's hard for most of us to even imagine. But before the vision is complete, God uses John to make at least one thing crystal clear.

And I heard a loud voice from the throne saying, "Behold, the dwelling place of God is with man. He will dwell with them, and they will be his people, and God himself will be with them as their God. He will wipe away every tear from their eyes, and death shall be no more, neither shall there be mourning, nor crying, nor pain anymore, **for the former things have passed away**." (Rev 21.3–4)

"Former things." Former things are in the past. They came before, and they are no more. Their time has come and gone. They are "former" things.

Child of God, your heavenly Father wants you to know that the day is coming when every tear, every experience of pain, every season of mourning, every temptation, every hardship, even death itself—all of the most painful things in the present—will be transformed into "former things."

> And he who was seated on the throne said, "Behold, I am making all things new." Also he said, "Write this down, for these words are trustworthy and true." (Rev 21.5)

And so we live, we endure, we grieve, we hope, and we press on by faith, trusting the testimony of the One who has conquered and promised to make all things new. We walk by faith in the present, fully assured of our future, because "the sufferings of this present time are not worth comparing with the glory that is to be revealed to us" (Rom 8.18).

One day, the worst sufferings of the present will be swallowed up in victory and all the saints of all the ages will look back on them from eternal glory as "former things."

Amen. Come, Lord Jesus!

# ALSO BY JASON HARDIN

## Boot Camp
*Equipping Men with Integrity for Spiritual Warfare*
Jason Hardin has a desire to equip the men of today to live lives of integrity. In his book, *Boot Camp: Equipping Men with Integrity for Spiritual Warfare,* he provides a Basic Training manual in spiritual warfare equipping men to fight for honor, integrity and a God-glorifying life.

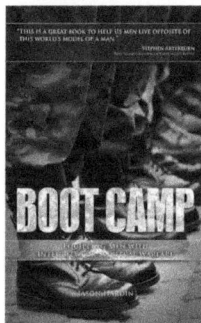

## Hard Core
*Defeating Sexual Temptation with a Superior Satisfaction*
*Hard Core* deals with how to defeat sexual temptation and find something more satisfying. So many—men *and* women—are being slaughtered in their struggle with sexual sin. Individual lives, marriages, children, influences for good, ministries of gospel preachers, and entire congregations of the Lord's people are being seriously impacted.

## Hello, I'm Your Bible
*A Practical Guide to Accurately Handling the Word of Truth*
*Hello, I'm Your Bible* is a practical guide to understanding and applying God's word of truth. Whether you've just been introduced to the Bible, you'd like to get reacquainted with the Scriptures, or you're looking to grow in your ability to help others in their walk of faith, *Hello, I'm Your Bible* can guide you into a deeper relationship with the God behind the living and active word.

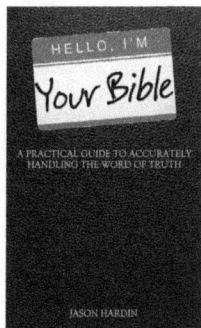

For a full listing of our books, visit DeWard's website:
**www.deward.com**

DeWard™
for your journey